Midwest Foraging for Beginners

Exploring the Natural Harvests of the Heartland Region – Your Essential Field Guide to Wild Edibles

Table of Contents

Introduction

Foraging is an ancient art that was a daily routine for your ancestors. Why pay for something you can collect yourself? By engaging in this art, you are saving money, getting exercise, and learning some survival knowledge in the process. The Midwest, especially, is ripe with plenty of foraging opportunities that will start a cycle of conservation and sustainability for you and the environment as you substantially contribute to reducing your carbon footprint.

In this book, you will learn to forage like a regular in the heartland of the United States. You will be taken through the bare basics as a beginner who knows nothing about foraging, from its historical significance to modern practical tips. *Why is the Midwest ideal for foraging? How can you respect and preserve the environment while enjoying its variety of offerings?*

In the second chapter, your practical foraging journey will begin. You'll find out which tools and equipment you'll need and what safety precautions you must take. Nature is wild and able to take care of itself. Before foraging, you must be prepared to tackle its natural defense mechanisms.

Then, you will take a close look at the heart of the Midwest, foraging for all its seasonal delights. Learn exactly which delicacies to look for at what time of the year. You don't want to end up with stale fruits for your homemade pie. However, what's the use of knowing which plants to forage at what time if you don't know what they look like? Your knowledge about each plant's appearance will be updated in the next chapter, including the most important food source of the Midwest - mushrooms.

Fresh wild edibles are delicious as they are, but you can make them taste even better using the sumptuous recipes discussed in this book. They will satisfy your appetite more than anything you have cooked or tasted with store-bought ingredients. Did you know you can also use certain plants and fruits to heal common illnesses and diseases?

Once you've made foraging a habit, leading the ideal foraging lifestyle won't be too difficult. The tips explained in the final chapter will help you considerably to incorporate your newfound skills into your daily routine. As an added bonus, this book includes a dedicated Midwest foraging calendar created by experts.

Foraging may seem like a difficult task that is reserved only for professionals in the field. However, the easy-to-understand information contained in this book will transform you into a foraging professional by lending you skills that will last you for a lifetime.

Chapter 1: Foraging in the Midwest: Getting Started as a Beginner

You may have only experienced bustling city life or explored quaint small towns of the Midwest. Still, look beyond its flourishing civilization. You will see vast rolling plains in Illinois and Ohio, dense forests dominated by formidable oaks and colorful maples in Wisconsin and Minnesota, shimmering lakes and gushing rivers in Missouri and Michigan, and boundless breathtaking prairies extending beyond Kansas and Nebraska's horizon.

Urban life is just a small part of the Midwest's diverse landscape, making it ideal for beginning your foraging journey. However, before we start - what is foraging in the first place? Is it a new concept for building a sustainable future? Can anyone and everyone do it?

A Brief History of Foraging

Foraging is the act of searching for and collecting food resources from the natural environment.[1]

Foraging is the act of searching for and collecting food resources from the natural environment. It involves several activities, from gathering wild plants to hunting animals. It can also be called foraging if you are looking for food in the refrigerator. However, this book focuses on foraging edible plants and fruits in the Midwest.

Most animals, including humans, cannot create their own food like plants do (photosynthesis). They are called *heterotrophs* (eating other organisms or plants) instead of *autotrophs* who can synthesize their own food (cooking doesn't count!). Ever since these heterotrophs first came into the world, they have been foraging for survival. You will learn this age-old survival technique to thrive in the modern world.

Specifically in the Midwest, foraging has been a part of human survival and culture throughout history. Indigenous peoples have practiced it for thousands of years, relying on the rich array of plant and animal resources found in the region's diverse ecosystems.

Native American tribes like the Ojibwe, Potawatomi, Ho-Chunk (Winnebago), Sioux, and many others have inhabited the Midwest for millennia. They had extensive knowledge of the local flora and fauna and used many plants and animals for food, medicine, clothing, tools, and shelter.

The indigenous peoples didn't just randomly collect and hoard any kind of plant life they could lay their hands on. They knew exactly which plants were edible and which were poisonous. They also knew that their natural resources were limited, so they were meticulous in managing their collection and cultivating more if required. Yes, the Native Americans may have been among the first to incorporate sustainable practices.

With the arrival of European settlers in the 17th and 18th centuries, foraging practices in the Midwest began to change. While Native American foraging traditions persisted among some groups, the Europeans introduced new plants and agricultural practices that altered the landscape and ecosystems of the region. Nevertheless, foraging for plants remained an essential supplement to farming and hunting for many people, especially those living on the frontier (the advancing border of the U.S.).

The practice saw a steep decline in the 19th and early 20th centuries because of the rapid industrialization and urbanization in the Midwest. As cities grew and agricultural practices intensified, many natural habitats were lost or degraded, reducing the availability of wild foods. Despite all these developments, a select few Indigenous, rural, and immigrant communities indulged in foraging.

In recent decades, more and more people have begun to realize the importance of this ancient activity across the U.S. These days, many individuals and households in the Midwest are now wholeheartedly embracing it. This renewed interest is primarily due to a growing awareness of wild foods' nutritional and ecological benefits and the rising preference for locally sourced and sustainably harvested foods.

People are rediscovering the abundance of edible and medicinal plants that grow wild in the Midwest as they gradually realize the need to return to their roots through foraging. This brings you to the next section.

An Overview of the Enchanting Nature of the Midwest

There is a reason why foraging is more prominent in the Midwest than in other parts of the U.S. Nature can never be more raw, wild, and diverse anywhere else. You can find unending plains and lush prairies, extensive forests and large bodies of water, and various types of wild plants, fruits, and other little organisms. It's heaven on earth for aspiring or experienced foragers.

Almost every natural part of the Midwest has many foraging opportunities. There are the prairies which, not too long ago, covered vast expanses of the region. These extensive grasslands have deep, rich soils that support many edible wildflowers and plants found nowhere else in the country. Many deer, chickens, and bird species roam the land and skies. Prairies are also home to the endangered bison.

If you end up in a forest, it will be filled with deciduous trees and shrubs that shed their leaves yearly. In the fall season, you can forage there to your heart's content without using special tools. You can find trees like oak, maple, and hickory, along with wildlife that includes many species of reptiles and amphibians.

The Great Lakes region in the Midwest.[a]

Then there's the Great Lakes region in the Midwest, where there is an abundance of options for foraging. It features five of the largest lakes in the U.S.: Superior to the west, Michigan, Huron, Erie, and Ontario to the far east. Except for Lake Ontario, all the other lakes are situated in the Midwest.

You don't have to dive into the lakes for foraging. The shores contain plenty of wild plants, fruits, and edible flowers. Wild mushrooms are specifically plentiful in the region. There are also many annual gatherings of foragers in the area who share their harvest and expertise. The wildlife includes migratory birds, turtles, and several fish species.

It doesn't have to be a wet shore for wild edibles to thrive. The region has many riparian zones and transitional areas between terrestrial and aquatic ecosystems. Trees like cottonwoods and willows grow there, which provide many foraging opportunities. The wildlife usually consists of mammals and amphibians.

If you want to forage for acorns while searching for variety in the prairies, you can head to the oak savannas of Minnesota, Missouri, and Illinois. Oak savannas contain oak trees in the prairies, a rare combination that provides the best of both worlds to the forager. They were naturally created in the past when lightning-caused wildfires in forests, leaving only the old oak trees standing.

Wetlands offer few foraging opportunities, but they cover vast swaths of land in the Midwest, so they are worth mentioning. Marshes, swamps, bogs, and floodplains play crucial ecological roles, such as water filtration, flood control, and habitat provision. Plants edible to humans may be scarce, but many animals, such as waterfowls, amphibians, and fish, thrive on the vegetation.

Quick Examples of Wild Edibles in the Midwest

The Midwest is home to a great variety of wild edibles, but mushrooms are commonly found almost everywhere in the region. There are the morel mushrooms *(Morchella)* that look like honeycombs. Morels are highly prized for their distinct flavor and are usually found in forests soon after spring. Chanterelle mushrooms *(Cantharellus)* look like funnel-shaped flowers. They have a fruity aroma and can be found near oak and pine trees.

- **Dandelion** *(Taraxacum officinale):* The entire plant is edible, including leaves, flowers, and roots. Dandelion greens are often used in salads or cooked like spinach.

- **Lamb's Quarters** *(Chenopodium album):* This nutritious plant is similar to spinach and can be eaten raw or cooked.

- **Purslane** *(Portulaca oleracea):* Purslane has succulent leaves that are high in omega-3 fatty acids. It can be eaten raw in salads or cooked as a vegetable.

- **Wild Strawberries** *(Fragaria virginiana):* These small, flavorful berries can be found in woodland edges and open fields.

- **Blackberries** *(Rubus):* Commonly found along roadsides, thickets, and forest edges, blackberries are delicious when ripe.

- **Mulberries** *(Morus):* Mulberries grow on trees and have a sweet flavor. They can be eaten fresh or used in jams and baked goods.

- **Black Walnuts** *(Juglans nigra):* Black walnuts have a robust flavor and can be gathered from trees in the fall. They are often used in baking.

- **Hickory Nuts** *(Carya):* Hickory nuts are another tasty option. They have a rich, buttery flavor and can be eaten raw or used in cooking.

- **Wild Asparagus** *(Asparagus officinalis):* Wild asparagus can be found in open fields or along roadsides, so you can forage for them while traveling to your environmental destination. It tastes richer than cultivated asparagus and can be cooked or eaten raw.

- **Wild Grapes** *(Vitis):* Several species of wild grapes grow in the Midwest, including riverbank grapes and fox grapes. They can be used to make jelly or wine or eaten fresh if ripe.

Practical Tips for Novices

Wild hemlock appears to be an innocent little flowering plant, but it is highly poisonous to humans.[9]

If you are new to the world of foraging, you can't just eat any plant that looks edible and tasty. For instance, the wild hemlock appears to be an innocent little flowering plant, but it is highly poisonous to humans. Safety is paramount for beginners. If you're unsure about the nature or characteristics of the plant, don't touch it.

However, it doesn't mean you should stay away from foraging altogether. You can make your way into this fascinating natural world with the help of the following practical tips:

- **Educate Yourself:** You may already be enchanted by the natural marvels of the Midwest, but don't start foraging just yet. Study the rest of the chapters in this book, know everything there is to know about the wild edibles in your area, browse through reputable foraging websites, and download apps to identify plants before venturing into the wild.

- **Start with Easy-to-Identify Species:** Focus on a few common, easily identifiable species with few or no toxic look-alikes. Dandelions, blackberries, and plantain are good options for beginners.

- **Know Where to Forage:** Seek out areas with minimal pollution and away from roadsides, industrial sites, and agricultural regions where pesticides might be present. Public parks, nature reserves, and forests are often good places to forage – but follow any rules or regulations regarding foraging in these areas.

- **Learn Plant Identification:** Focus on the key features of the plants, such as leaf shape, arrangement, color, and growth habits. Note any distinguishing characteristics, like flowers, berries, or unique markings. Always be 100% sure of the plant breed before eating it.

- **Harvest Ethically and Sustainably:** Only take what you need and leave enough behind to ensure the continued growth and reproduction of the species. Avoid harvesting rare or endangered plants, and be mindful of the ecosystem you're foraging in.

- **Use Proper Tools:** Bring a pair of scissors or a small knife for harvesting plants and a basket or bag to carry your finds. Avoid using plastic bags, as your delicate greens may wilt inside.

- **Be Aware of Seasonality:** Different wild edibles have specific seasons when they are ripe for harvesting. Pay attention to seasonal patterns and only harvest plants, fruits, or mushrooms when they are at their peak.

- **Start Slowly and Test New Foods:** Introduce wild edibles into your diet gradually, especially if you have allergies or sensitivities. Try small amounts of new foods first to ensure they agree with you, and don't eat anything you're uncertain about.

- **Join a Foraging Group:** Foragers often meet regularly in many parts of the Midwest. Connecting with experienced foragers in your community can provide valuable guidance, support, and opportunities for hands-on learning. You can also look for online forums or social media groups.

- **Respect Nature and Leave No Trace:** Leave the foraging area as you found it without damaging plants or disrupting wildlife. Practice "Leave No Trace" principles by properly disposing of waste and minimizing environmental impact.

Importance of Reliable Field Guides

You don't have to start foraging alone, especially as a beginner. This book will be your guide throughout your journey. You can look for other field guides to expand your knowledge, but make sure they are reliable books written by reputable authors with hands-on experience in foraging.

- Field guides provide detailed descriptions, photographs, or illustrations of wild plants, mushrooms, and berries, helping you accurately identify species in the wild. Proper identification is crucial for distinguishing edible plants from toxic look-alikes and ensuring a safe foraging experience.

- Foraging field guides include details and statistics about the edibility and toxicity of wild plants and flowers. These guides will help you avoid harmful plants or mushrooms and minimize the risk of accidental poisoning.

- They include all the information about the seasonal availability and preferred habitats of wild edibles. Understanding when and where to find specific plants or mushrooms increases the chances of successful foraging outings.

- They offer practical tips and techniques for foraging, including harvesting methods, preparation instructions, and recipe ideas. The tips you learned in the previous section will be discussed in detail in the following chapters. They will help you enhance your foraging skills and experience diverse culinary experiences.

- Reliable field guides cover a wide range of plant and mushroom species found in a particular region or ecosystem. This specific and comprehensive coverage allows you to explore every type of known edible available in your area and discover new species in the future.

- They are compact, lightweight books that are easy to carry in a backpack or pocket during foraging outings. They provide on-the-go reference materials you can consult when encountering unfamiliar plants or flowers in the field.

- Having a reliable field guide by your side can boost your confidence in your foraging abilities. You can quickly reference information and confirm identifications to avoid accidentally pulling out the wrong flower or a poisonous mushroom.

Ethical Considerations of Foraging

You pay money when you want something from a store. If you take it without paying anything, it's called stealing. Similarly, in the foraging world, you are taking something from the natural environment. Isn't it your responsibility to give something back?

The plants and mushrooms you pluck are living, breathing organisms. They don't understand the concept of money or trade, but it doesn't mean you should keep taking it. It benefits neither them nor you. They may one day become extinct, and with them goes your food source. This is why there are a few solid ethical rules that every forager should follow.

- **Respect for Nature:** You should approach nature with reverence and appreciation, recognizing that you are a guest in their ecosystem. Respect the plants, animals, and habitats encountered while foraging. Don't harm or disrupt their way of life.

- **Sustainable Harvesting:** Harvest wild edibles sustainably, taking only what is needed and leaving enough behind to support plant growth and reproduction. Avoid over-harvesting rare or slow-growing species and focus on abundant and resilient plants. Don't harvest any endangered species.

- **Native Plant Preservation:** Prioritize the conservation of native plant species by keeping them abundant and avoiding planting non-native or invasive species in the area. Be careful of the potential ecological impacts of foraging on native plant communities and habitats.

- **Responsible Foraging Practices:** Follow ethical guidelines, such as obtaining permission before foraging on private property, respecting designated conservation areas and protected lands, and adhering to local regulations and harvesting limits.

- **Leave No Trace:** Practice Leave No Trace principles by minimizing your impact on the environment during foraging outings. Pack out any trash or litter, avoid trampling sensitive shrubs and plants, and don't interfere with the wildlife or nesting areas.

- **Cultural Respect:** Respect the cultural significance of wild edibles to indigenous communities and traditional cultures. Explore their relation to Native American practices and avoid appropriating or exploiting cultural resources.

- **Stay Updated:** Since foraging has recently gained momentum in the Midwest, the practices and ethical considerations are constantly evolving. Keep yourself updated about the ecological, cultural, and ethical dimensions of foraging. Explore the local conservation efforts, invasive species management, and sustainable harvesting practices, and share this knowledge with your family and friends to promote ethical foraging practices.

- **Community Engagement:** Go beyond the people you know and engage with local communities, conservation organizations, and foraging groups. Share your knowledge and learn in return. Participate in volunteer activities, educational events, and conservation initiatives that support the ethical practice of foraging.

The ecosystem is delicately balanced on a fragile scale. If you take something out, be prepared to maintain the balance by following all ethical practices. The scale is already leaning toward destruction, thanks to the increased pollution and the global warming threat. Don't accelerate its downfall any further.

A Journey of Connection with Nature

There is an ancient Native American saying, *"The Great Spirit is in all things. He is in the air we breathe. The Great Spirit is our Father, but the Earth is our Mother. She nourishes us. That which we put into the ground; she returns to us."*

Nurturing is a two-way street. If you care for the environment, the environment will take care of you by giving you plenty of foraging opportunities. In this sense, foraging is more than just a hobby. It is a way of life that should be heartily embraced. Treat nature like a long-lost friend, and it will stand by you through the fiercest of storms.

Foraging gives you free food and helps you forge a bond with the environment. You learn to develop a heightened awareness of seasonal changes as you observe wild edibles' emergence, growth, and decline throughout the year. This awareness of the seasonal rhythms will become instinctual with time and practice.

Did you know the act of foraging utilizes all your senses? The sight of vibrant wildflowers, the scent of fresh herbs, the touch of textured leaves, the sound of rustling foliage, and the taste of ripe berries will improve your senses and help you develop a deeper connection with nature.

When you start foraging, your curiosity will be at an all-time high. It will help you take a keen interest in your surroundings, identifying and learning about different plant species, habitats, and ecosystems. You will understand and appreciate the raw power of nature and the beautiful diversity of its offerings.

If you've heard about mindfulness techniques, you will know they are the art of being one with your surroundings. Foraging makes you one with nature without needing to practice special mindfulness techniques. You will experience all the benefits of mindfulness, from basic mental and physical relaxation to the joy of living a stress-free life.

Indigenous foragers develop a personal relationship with the plants they harvest, recognizing them as more than just food sources but as living beings with unique characteristics, life cycles, and ecological roles. As John Fire Lame Deer of the Heyoka society once said, *"A good way to start thinking about nature, talk about it. Rather talk to it, talk to the rivers, to the lakes, to the winds as to our relatives."*

Furthermore, foraging promotes a sense of environmental stewardship and responsibility as you develop a deeper understanding of natural ecosystems' ecological dynamics and conservation needs. This stewardship will inspire you to follow ethical practices naturally without referring to this book.

Remember this meaningful Native American quote, *"We do not inherit the Earth from our Ancestors; we borrow it from our Children."* Forage for yourself and your family, but leave plenty for future generations.

Chapter 2: Foraging Tools, Equipment, and Safety

While foraging is an excellent activity to connect to the wild and reap nature's bounty spread, getting ready properly and being careful when you're out foraging is essential. It's all about staying safe and ensuring you're not harming nature. Knowing what dangers to look for and having the right gear keeps you safe. Besides having gear and tools, there are rules to follow – like keeping yourself hydrated, using tools effectively, and being thoughtful and respectful while foraging, which keeps nature healthy and enjoyable. Furthermore, knowing which plants are safe and which aren't is essential so you don't accidentally eat something poisonous. In this chapter, you will read about safety, foraging tools, potential hazards you might encounter, and the rules you must follow to keep you safe during your foraging adventures.

Understanding the Terrain

Understanding and preparing for the diverse terrain of the Midwest will make your foraging expeditions safe and enjoyable.[4]

Understanding and preparing for the diverse terrain of the Midwest will make your foraging expeditions safe and enjoyable. The Midwest region includes various landscapes with particular characteristics and potential risks.

Flat Plains

You'll find vast flat plains in States like Illinois and Iowa. While these areas may seem relatively easy to navigate, you must be aware of hazards like uneven ground, hidden holes or depressions, and agricultural machinery. In this terrain, picking proper footwear, carrying only necessary gear, and paying attention to surroundings are key to avoiding accidents.

Wooded Areas

Michigan and Wisconsin have dense forests and wooded areas. Foragers exploring these regions should be prepared for thick vegetation and fallen branches and potentially encountering wildlife like snakes or poisonous insects. As the field of view is limited in dense woodlands, carrying a map or GPS device can prevent you from getting lost, while wearing sturdy clothing and taking safety measures to deter wildlife can keep you protected.

River Valleys and Wetlands

Throughout the Midwest, river valleys and wetlands provide a rich ecosystem for foraging. However, these areas also have risks like slippery terrain, sudden water level changes, and poisonous plants. To forage in this terrain, always be cautious when navigating near bodies of water, wear appropriate footwear for wet conditions, and be mindful of common poisonous plants like poison ivy or oak.

Rolling Hills

Parts of Ohio and Indiana feature rolling hills and valleys, which can present challenges for foragers, especially in steep inclines and declines. Footwear with good traction is essential for navigating these terrains safely, and carrying walking sticks or trekking poles gives added stability on uneven ground.

Urban and Suburban Areas

Wild plants and mushrooms can grow even in urban and suburban settings in parks and green spaces. However, you must be mindful of potential hazards like polluted soil, pesticide use, and regulations regarding foraging on public or private property.

This is a basic introduction to the terrains you will encounter in the Midwest region. Each terrain has several features worth studying. Research the terrain you will be foraging in, anticipate potential risks associated with the landscape, and adequately prepare yourself with the necessary equipment for a safe and enjoyable foraging experience. Furthermore, you must learn the required foraging skills and the proper use of foraging tools, and you must always carry navigation gadgets. Remember to be aware of local regulations as well.

Essential Foraging Tools

Foraging in the wild requires a few essential tools to make it a successful and enjoyable experience. Here are some indispensable tools you will need for your foraging adventures.

Quality Knife

A quality knife is a versatile tool for harvesting plants, cutting through tough stems, and processing wild edibles. Choose a knife with a sturdy blade and comfortable grip for extended use. Keep it sharp and well-maintained for use during foraging expeditions.

Practical Tip: Practice proper knife safety techniques, like keeping the blade away from your body and using controlled, precise cuts to avoid accidents.

Sturdy Foraging Bag

A foraging bag is necessary to collect and transport your foraged materials safely.[5]

A foraging bag is necessary to collect and transport your foraged materials safely. These bags come in a variety of shapes, sizes, and compartments. A foraging bag with ample space, durable materials, and comfortable carrying straps can do the trick. Mesh compartments or pockets in your foraging back can make it easier to organize different foraged items and prevent delicate plants from getting crushed.

However, if you go old school and want to use the traditional foraging basket, line it with a cloth to cushion fragile items and avoid moisture buildup.

Gloves

Protect your hands from thorns, prickles, and potential irritants with gloves.'

Protect your hands from thorns, prickles, and potential irritants with gloves. Choose foraging gloves made of a solid but thin material that provides better touch sensitivity and allows easy hand movements to handle plants safely.

Practical Tip: Choose gloves made from breathable materials to prevent sweat buildup and ensure comfort during long foraging trips.

Fuel for the Body

Carry a reusable water bottle and nutritious snacks to stay hydrated and energized. Choose lightweight, portable items that won't weigh you down but provide essential hydration and sustenance to keep you going.

Practical Tip: Pack snacks that are easy to eat on the go, like nuts, dried fruits, trail mixes, or energy bars, to replenish energy levels and stave off hunger.

You can add various other foraging tools to your foraging gear for a streamlined experience. These include the following:

- **Pruners:** This tool is mainly used to process herbs and can snip through stems, roots, twigs, and small branches.

- **Kitchen Scissors:** Best for foraging stemmed greens like chickweed *(Stellaria media)*, cleavers *(Galium aparine)*, etc.

- **Pruning Saw:** A foldable pruning saw is handy when foraging medium-sized tree branches, such as wild cherry tree barks for medicinal purposes.

- **Leather Holster:** Foragers use leather holsters to carry tools safely. These holsters can be custom-made to their preferences and the number of tools they will use.

- **Hand Trowel:** Carry a small hand trowel to loosen the soil and harvest root vegetables or tubers, carefully extracting the plants without causing damage.

- **Multi-Tool:** Consider carrying a multi-tool with built-in features like a knife, scissors, and tweezers for various tasks during foraging expeditions. Choose a lightweight and compact design for convenience.

The choice of tools you need will depend on your goals. For example, if you want to forage mushrooms, a sturdy and sharp knife and a foraging bag work. However, if you plan to forage wild berries on the trip, tucking in a pruner alongside your knife will make foraging much easier. You can tweak what tools you carry with you according to your personal preferences and foraging requirements.

Prioritize Safety

Safety should always be the top priority during outdoor activities, including foraging. Be aware of risks so you know how to navigate potential hazards and minimize the likelihood of accidents or injuries. Here are some guidelines to keep you safe:

- **Know Before You Go:** Research the area you plan to forage in, including terrain features, local wildlife, poisonous plants, or dangerous animals you might encounter.

- **Stay Alert:** Stay vigilant while foraging, looking for uneven ground, slippery surfaces, sharp objects (rocks, tree barks, etc.), or other obstacles that could cause trips or falls. Check the weather conditions before heading out.

- **Use Proper Equipment:** Always pack appropriate gear. This will include appropriate footwear for the terrain, protective gloves, a first aid kit, a bag, foraging tools, and navigation tools like a map or GPS device. Only use equipment that is in good condition and well-maintained to avoid malfunctions or accidents.

- **Practice Tool Usage:** Whether you want to use a knife, pruner, or some other tool to harvest plants, always handle it carefully and follow proper safety protocols. Keep the sharp edges pointed away from yourself and others, and use controlled motions to avoid accidental cuts or injuries.

- **Stay Hydrated and Nourished:** Bring a sufficient water supply and nutritious snacks to keep yourself hydrated and energized during your foraging expedition. Dehydration and fatigue impair judgment and increase the risk of accidents. For example, if you are going out for a three-hour foraging expedition, pack at least a liter of water and two energy bars so you don't get drowsy or experience fatigue.

- **Buddy System:** If possible, forage with a companion or in a group. Having someone with you takes the experience to another level and ensures an extra set of eyes and hands in emergencies.

- **Respect Nature and Wildlife:** When foraging, respect the natural environment and its inhabitants. Avoid disturbing wildlife, stay on designated trails or paths, and never leave waste or litter.

- **Know Your Limits:** Be honest about your physical abilities and limitations. Never push yourself beyond your capabilities and only step outside your comfort zone or attempt to tackle challenging terrain if you're adequately prepared. Listen to your body and know when to take a break or call it a day.

Potential Hazards

Now that you know your terrain and have the required foraging gear, the next thing to work on is getting around potential hazards you can encounter. Here are some common hazards to help you understand how to handle these challenges effectively:

Poisonous Plants

In the Midwest, common poisonous plants include poison ivy, poison oak, and wild parsnip. Learn to distinguish them from harmless look-alikes by studying their leaf patterns and growth habits. For example, poison ivy has clusters of three shiny leaflets, and you must avoid contact. Furthermore, when foraging in areas where these plants are prevalent, like forested regions or meadows, stay on marked trails and avoid touching unfamiliar plants.

If you accidentally touch a poisonous plant, rinse the affected area with soap and water to remove plant oils. Seek medical attention if a rash or other symptoms, like a skin-burning sensation, itching, or redness, develop.

Dangerous Terrain

Study topographic maps to understand the landscape before exploring rugged terrains like hilly areas or rocky outcrops. If you plan to forage in a rocky area, avoid loose rocks or areas that look like unstable footing. Invest in sturdy hiking boots with ankle support and grippy soles for traction on uneven surfaces.

Don't forget that proper footwear prevents slips and falls when crossing muddy trails or slippery rocks near streams. Take your time navigating challenging terrain, and always use trekking poles when ascending steep slopes to maintain balance and stability.

Additional Precautions

Keep an eye on weather forecasts before heading out foraging. If thunderstorms are predicted, avoid open areas or high ground where you could be at risk of lightning strikes. No matter the weather, pack a first aid kit with bandages, antiseptic wipes, and tweezers to remove splinters or thorns. Remember to throw in a fully charged cell phone or satellite communicator in emergencies.

Clothing Preferences

Appropriate clothing will keep you comfortable, protected, and safe during expeditions. Here are the essentials of your foraging gear:

Sturdy Footwear

Choose hiking boots with ankle support and a good tread pattern to maintain stability on uneven terrain.[7]

- **Hiking Boots:** Choose hiking boots with ankle support and a good tread pattern to maintain stability on uneven terrain and protect your feet from sharp rocks or roots.

- **Waterproofing:** Consider waterproof or water-resistant footwear, especially when foraging in wet or muddy conditions, to keep the feet dry and prevent discomfort and blisters.

Ensure your boots fit well and have enough room for your toes to wiggle without feeling too loose. Try them on with hiking socks to ensure a comfortable fit.

Clothing Layers

- **Base Layer:** To keep sweat away from your skin, start with moisture-wicking clothing, like synthetic or merino wool shirts and pants.

- **Insulating Layer:** Add insulating layers like fleece jackets or vests to trap body heat in colder weather. Choose lightweight, breathable materials when foraging in hot conditions.

- **Outer Shell:** Wear a waterproof and windproof outer shell, like a rain jacket and pants, to protect against rain, wind, and moisture. Look for garments with adjustable hoods and cuffs for a snug fit.

Protective Gear

- **Gloves:** Choose durable gloves with grip-enhancing palms for handling tools and plants safely.

- **Hat:** Protect your head and face from sunburn and heatstroke by wearing a wide-brimmed hat or a baseball cap with a neck flap.

- **Sunglasses:** Invest in UV-protective sunglasses to shield your eyes from harmful sun rays and reduce glare when foraging in bright sunlight. Look for polarized lenses for enhanced visibility and better eye protection.

- **Insect Repellent:** Apply insect repellent containing DEET or picaridin to exposed skin to ward off mosquitoes, ticks, and other biting insects. Reapply as directed, especially in heavily infested areas.

- **Seasonal Adaptations:** Adjust your clothing choices based on the season and weather conditions. For example, wear breathable fabrics in summer to stay cool and use lightweight thermal layers in winter to retain heat.

- **High-Visibility Gear:** If you're foraging near roads or in areas with hunting activity, wear brightly colored clothing or reflective gear to increase visibility and reduce the risk of accidents.

- **Carrying Comfort:** Choose gear that isn't restrictive and allows for freedom of movement. Use a comfortable backpack or foraging bag and distribute weight evenly to prevent strain.

Magnifying Glass

Tuck in a handheld magnifying glass to examine intricate details of plants, like leaf veins, flower structures, and related features, for better plant identification. Seeing through a magnifying glass can also reveal the presence of insects.

With a magnifying glass, you can also observe the world of tiny organisms up close. Many insects, larvae, and fungal spores can be spotted easily, giving you a closer look at the intricate web of life within the natural environment.

Containers for Safe Transport

As mentioned, use a sturdy foraging bag or basket with ample space to safely transport your harvested items without crushing them. Look for designs with breathable materials and compartments to separate different foraged goods. You can also use separate mesh bags to collect delicate items like berries or mushrooms, allowing airflow to prevent spoilage. These mesh bags can also be used for easy rinsing if you want to try the foraged produce on the spot.

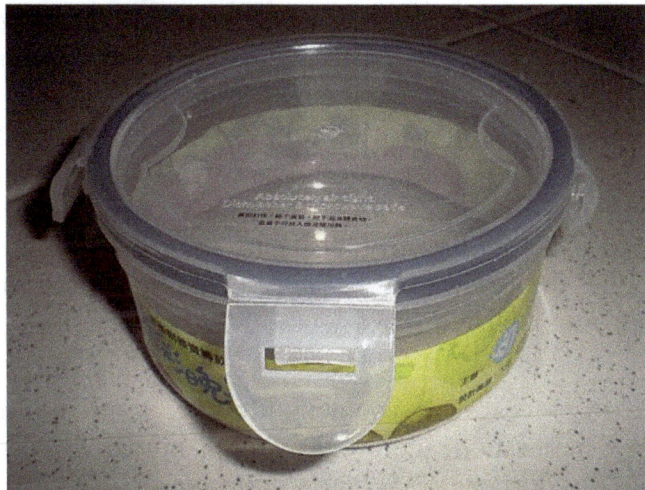

Store easily damaged plants, wild berries, or greens in airtight containers to keep them fresh.'

- **Airtight Containers:** Store easily damaged plants and wild berries or greens in airtight containers to keep them fresh and prevent spoilage during transport. Choose lightweight, BPA-free containers that are easy to pack and carry.

- **Waterproof Bags:** Pack waterproof bags or pouches to protect your gadgets, documents, or valuables from moisture during rainy weather or water crossings.

Maintaining Tools

Cleaning

After each foraging trip, clean your tools thoroughly to remove any dirt, sap, or residue that may have accumulated. Use a soft-bristled toothbrush or paintbrush to dislodge debris from hard-to-reach areas. For stubborn dirt or sticky substances, use a mild soap solution and warm water to scrub the surfaces of your tools gently.

Avoid harsh chemicals or abrasive cleaners that could damage the metal or finishes. Once cleaned, completely dry them before storing them to prevent rust or corrosion. Use a clean, dry cloth to wipe them down, and allow them to air dry in a well-ventilated area.

Sharpening

The frequency of sharpening depends on usage and the type of tool, but a good rule of thumb is to sharpen knives and cutting tools after every few uses or when they start to feel dull. You can use sharpening stones, honing rods, or sharpening systems to maintain a sharp edge on your tools. Practice proper sharpening techniques to achieve optimal results, like keeping a consistent angle and even pressure.

After sharpening, test the sharpness of your tools by carefully running them across a piece of paper or cardboard. A sharp edge should make a clean cut without snagging or tearing the material. You can also achieve a razor-sharp edge by adding stropping into your sharpening routine. It involves running the blade over a leather or fabric surface impregnated with abrasive compounds.

Storage

Choose a dry storage environment for your tools to prevent rust, corrosion, or deterioration, and avoid damp or humid areas, as moisture can promote rust formation. When storing, never overcrowd or stack tools on top of each other, as this can lead to scratches, dents, or other forms of damage. A tool rack, pegboard, or drawer organizer to keep your tools organized and easily accessible. Arrange them according to size or function to streamline your workflow and minimize searching time.

Inspection

Inspect your tools regularly for any wear, damage, or malfunction. Pay particular attention to blade edges, handles, and pivot points. Look for signs of dullness, chipping, rust, loose screws, or cracks that may indicate the need for maintenance or repair.

Test the functionality of moving parts, locking mechanisms, or other features to ensure smooth operation. Check that everything is working properly.

Proper Use

Follow manufacturer recommendations and guidelines for properly using and maintaining your tools. Refer to user manuals or online resources for specific care instructions tailored to each tool type. Furthermore, handle the tools carefully and avoid excessive force or strain to prevent accidents or injury.

Proper Care for Specialty Tools

Although most tools used foraging are easy to care for and maintain, if you are a budding naturalist and are into gathering keepsakes for nature, you might use specialty tools like botanical specimen collection kits. Besides reviewing the manufacturer guidelines or seeking advice from knowledgeable sources for proper care and handling, invest your time researching best practices for maintaining specialty tools. You can also attend workshops, seminars, or online courses to expand your knowledge and skills in caring for specialized gear.

Environmental Considerations

While maintaining and storing your tools after each use can increase their longevity, here are a few environmental factors you must know.

Climate Adaptation

Consider temperature, humidity, and exposure to sunlight when storing or maintaining your tools. Extreme conditions can accelerate wear, degradation, or deterioration, forcing you to take extra protective measures.

Seasonal Adjustments

Adjust your maintenance routine annually according to changes in weather or environmental conditions. For example, increase ventilation during high humidity or use dehumidifiers to prevent moisture-related issues like rust or mold growth.

The connection between safety, proper tools, and an enjoyable foraging experience is undeniable. You can enjoy your foraging expeditions with confidence and peace of mind by prioritizing safety and carrying the right tools and knowledge.

Throughout this chapter, you've uncovered essential foraging tools, safety precautions, and maintenance tips to help you navigate the wild with ease and effectiveness. Each tool, from reliable field guides and quality knives to sturdy footwear and protective gear, enhances safety and efficiency during foraging.

While you've gathered your tools and honed your skills to become a skilled forager, it's vital to remember that the essence of an exemplary forager lies in the care for oneself and the environment. Always stay vigilant to potential risks, honor nature's abundance, and adhere to responsible foraging practices. This mindful approach ensures your safety and the preservation of natural ecosystems. Embrace these practices to keep your adventures safe and sustain your deep connection with the natural world for many years!

Chapter 3: Seasonal Foraging in the Midwest

As the seasons change, the foraging landscape changes as well. Different wild plants grow throughout the year, allowing you to experiment with various edibles and flavors. This chapter covers the unique edible plants that grow each season in the Midwest and provides some harvesting tips and techniques to gather the plants safely and sustainably.

The Cyclical Nature in the Midwest

Equatorial countries, among other places worldwide, only have two seasons, which prevents various plants from growing in these regions. The rest of the world experiences different weather cycles that contribute to leaves changing and the blooming of a wide range of plants during each season. For instance, winter buds open in the spring, and the poinsettia flower grows during the winter.

The Midwest is known for its humid climate, which includes frigid winters and sweltering summers. Plants that grow in this region should be strong enough to withstand low temperatures, such as oyster mushrooms, and severe heat, such as purslane, which can adjust to different climates.

A unique variety of plants bloom in the Midwest throughout the year thanks to its weather, which can be hot, warm, cool, and cold.

Spring

Spring is the season of renewal, as nature finally awakens from its long winter slumber.'

Spring is the season of renewal, as nature finally awakens from its long winter slumber. The world changes its colors as flowers and other plants emerge during this time. Embrace this special time by foraging spring wild edibles through the Midwest's diverse landscape.

The best forageable spring plants in the Midwest are greens, shoots, and mushrooms.

Greens

Dandelion: It can be found all over the Midwest since it grows in any cultivated land, especially grass.

Harvesting Techniques and Tips

- Harvest dandelion leaves in early spring, preferably after dawn, and pick them by hand or use pruners.

- Young leaves are usually delicious, while mature ones are perfect for sauteed recipes.

- Cover the flowers with a dark cloth to blanch them before harvesting to reduce the bitterness.

- Harvest the dandelion flower blossoms in mid or late spring by plucking them by hand.

- Pick the flowers when they start opening before the petals fall. Put the stems in cool water to keep them fresh.
- Harvest the roots anytime during the year by digging them up with your hands. Large roots in well-drained soil are easier to remove than small roots in dry soil. In this case, you will need a shovel. Wash the roots before using them.

Ramps: These usually grow in woodland and forests in the Midwest and last for a month or less, making them less available than other spring plants.

Harvesting Techniques and Tips

- Harvest ramps in mid-spring.
- Harvest by taking a small piece of the bulb. Insert a knife into the dirt or dig with a shovel and cut it off, but leave a big part – or the roots will not grow.
- Ramps usually take up to 15 years to reach optimal growth. Overharvested patches can take years to grow back, so practice sustainable harvest by taking only 20% of each ramp colony.
- Pick ramps from different areas to give them space to breathe.
- Ramps have a more robust flavor than regular leeks, so only use a small amount in recipes.

Wild Garlic Mustard: This is widely available in the Midwest and usually grows in forests, wooded areas, waste places, gardens, lawns, meadows, pastures, grain fields, and along streams and roads.

Harvesting Technique and Tips

- Harvest wild garlic mustard in mid-spring during the plant's second year when flower buds grow on top of the plant and the stems are thick and succulent.
- Snap off the stems' tender part, about 6 to 12 inches, with your fingers.
- Harvest the leaves in the first year by cutting them off with your hands or pruning shears.
- Dry them and use them for seasoning.

Shoots

Asparagus is available in multiple Midwest states.[10]

Asparagus: It is available in multiple Midwest states, such as Ohio, Illinois, Wisconsin, and Michigan – *the top asparagus producer in the U.S.!*

Harvesting Techniques and Tips

- Harvest asparagus by sliding a knife down until you reach the stem and cutting it off slowly.

- Only cut the newly sprouted asparagus.

Nettles: These grow in temperate regions such as southwest Wisconsin on roadsides, ditches, hedgerows, woods, mountain slopes, and streams.

Harvesting Technique

1. Put on sturdy leather gloves.
2. Cut off the tender young plants' upper leaves using scissors.
3. Separate them from the stalks, then put them in a plastic bag.

Harvesting Tips

- Harvest nettles in mid or late spring.

- Wear gloves, as nettles have tiny hairs that sting.

- Cook nettles to destroy their stinging-forming acid.

- They shouldn't be eaten raw, so don't put them on your salad.

Burdocks: They grow all over the Midwest along waste areas, pastures, roadsides, and ditch banks.

Harvesting Techniques and Tips

- Harvest burdocks in mid-spring or when they are fully grown.
- Harvest the leaves when tender and young before they become too large.
- Loosen the soil below the ground to harvest the roots.
- Dig a hole using a garden fork or a shovel and gently pull out the root.

Sorrels: They grow all over the Midwest, especially in Minnesota. They grow in the woods and along parking lots.

Harvesting Techniques and Tips

- Harvest anytime during the spring.
- Harvest sorrels when the plant is about six inches tall.
- Look for the largest outer leaves.
- Cut off a quarter of the leaves with scissors to allow new leaves to grow.

Mushrooms

Morels usually grow in the woody edges of forests and around decaying apple trees, poplar, ash, and elms.[11]

Morels: These are common in the Midwest, especially in North and South Dakota, Minnesota, Wisconsin, Iowa, and Michigan. They usually grow in the woody edges of forests and around decaying apple trees, poplar, ash, and elms.

Harvesting Techniques and Tips

- Harvest morels in mid-spring.
- Cut the morel with a sharp knife above the ground and leave a small part of the stem.
- You can also twist the mushroom with your hand at the stem's base and pull it from the ground.
- All wild mushrooms are harvested using the same technique.

Wood Ear: They grow all over this region; look for them on decayed shrubs, trees, and conifer logs.

Harvesting Tips

- Harvest wood ear mushrooms in early spring.
- They grow in size underwater, so finding and harvesting them will be easier after the rain.

Summer

Summer is many people's favorite season. It is a time for unwinding, relaxation, and spending the day on the beach. The season is also special for gardeners as plants grow faster and stronger. The sun shines longer during the summer, providing the plants with enough sunlight for photosynthesis, which boosts their energy and encourages their growth. Tiny seedlings start growing and flowering, and some begin to fruit.

The abundance of wild edibles peaks during the summer when various types of berries, greens, and nuts grow.

Wild Strawberries: Grow all over the U.S. except for Hawaii, in woodlands, forest edges, and grasslands.

Harvesting Techniques and Tips

- Harvest wild strawberries in early summer.
- Snip the stems gently with your fingers instead of pulling the berry, or twist and pull the berries.
- Put the stems in a shallow container to prevent squashing the strawberries.

- Harvest early in the morning while the weather is cool, as the fruit will be firm and less likely to be damaged.

Black Raspberries: Grow throughout the Midwest, especially in the wild. They are low-yield and aren't as widely available as other summer plants.

Harvesting Techniques and Tips

- Harvest wild black raspberries in early summer.
- Wear old clothes. Black raspberry juice can stain them, and the thorns may rip them. Also, wear gloves to protect your hands from the thorns.
- Black raspberries don't ripen simultaneously. You will have to harvest them often.
- Harvest by picking the dark berries from the stems; they should easily fall off when ripe.
- Don't harvest berries that are hard to pull.
- Red berries are unripe and shouldn't be harvested. Wait until they turn black.

Huckleberries: They grow all over the Midwest in glades, open woods, cherts, and acid soil.

Harvesting Techniques and Tips

- Harvest huckleberries in mid-summer.
- Hold the stem with your fingers, gently twist it, and the ripe berries will fall.
- Put a container right under the plant so the berries fall into it.
- Handle the berries carefully, as they are fragile and can easily be crushed.
- Avoid using mechanical tools or rakes, as they can damage the plants.
- Don't harvest green berries and leave them to ripen.
- Ripe huckleberries are usually found on high branches.

Blueberries: They grow in the upper Midwest in Minnesota and Wisconsin. They grow abundantly in the U.S. since it is the world's largest producer of blueberries.

Harvesting Techniques and Tips

- Harvest blueberries in mid or late summer.
- Avoid harvesting when the plant is wet from morning dew or rain.
- Pick the berries gently with your fingers and collect them in a basket or a bowl.
- Don't overfill the basket, as blueberries are easily bruised and can squash.
- Don't leave them in the sun.
- Wash your hands before and after picking the berries.

Nuts

Black walnuts are harvested in the late summer.[13]

Black Walnuts: They grow in the Midwest, especially in Michigan, Minnesota, Illinois, Wisconsin, and Missouri.

Harvesting Techniques and Tips

- Harvest black walnuts in late summer.
- Pick the fallen nuts from the ground before the squirrels get to them.
- Ground nuts are safe, and the fall doesn't affect the nutmeat.
- You can also harvest the nuts on the trees using a hook on a long pole or shaking the tree, which will cause ripe nuts to fall.

- Black walnuts can stain, so wear gloves for protection.
- Remove the nuts' outer covering right after harvest, or they will turn black and decompose.

Filberts: Also called hazelnuts, filberts are found throughout the Midwest, especially in Illinois, Iowa, Minnesota, and Wisconsin. They usually grow in open fields and savannahs.

Harvesting Techniques and Tips

- Harvest filberts in late summer.
- If the filberts start to drop, gently shake the branches, and they will fall to the ground.
- Collect the nuts and put them in a basket.
- Some of the nuts may be empty or have worms. Put them in a large bowl of water. Bad nuts will float. Discard them right away. Use this technique to test all nut types.
- Throw away any nuts with holes, as they can be infested with insects.
- Hazelnuts have sharp hairs, so wear gloves to protect your hands.

Greens

Lamb's Quarters: These grow in the Midwest – Iowa, Minnesota, Illinois, Indiana, Wisconsin, and Nebraska.

Harvesting Techniques and Tips

- Harvest lamb's quarters in mid-summer, during the hottest months. The seeds should be black, and the flowers should be dry and brown.
- The plants should be six to eight inches tall when ready for harvest.
- Harvest by gently plucking the plant's tender tips with your fingers.

Purslane: This grows throughout the Midwest in distributed soil, sidewalk cracks, and gravel.

Harvesting Techniques and Tips

- Harvest purslane when it is six to eight weeks old - when the leaves are bright green and the stems are robust.
- Don't pick wilted or discolored leaves.

- Harvest early in the morning before the heat and after the dew evaporates.
- Cut the green parts with scissors, but leave the roots in the ground for sustainable harvest.
- You can also gently snip or pull the stem with scissors or a sharp life.

Summer Harvesting Techniques and Tips

- Some plants can be picked early or after they ripen. Know the right time for harvesting. Some summer plants can't tolerate high temperatures and may wither if left for too long in the heat.
- Harvest early in the morning when plants are hydrated and the weather is cool.
- Cut instead of tearing the plants to prevent bruising the fruit or vegetable and to avoid damaging the roots. Use scissors or a knife.
- Gently snip the vegetables, fruits, or berries without disturbing or damaging other parts.
- Put the plants you collect in a basket or a big bowl to protect them from bruising.
- Water the roots before harvesting to soften the soil and prevent plant skin damage.

Fall

During the fall, leaves change color, and many flowers dry out and stop blooming. However, the world doesn't remain colorless. Other types of flowers, like sunflowers and even roses, still bloom.

During the fall, the weather changes, and the days get shorter. Many trees stop producing chlorophyll, which transforms sunlight into energy. As a result, leaves change from green to orange and yellow.

Many wild plants also change colors during the fall as they come to life, allowing them to discover and forage new types of edible plants, such as fruits, nuts, seeds, and berries.

Fruits

Pawpaws: Grow in the wild and along streams in Midwest states such as Kansas, Nebraska, and Michigan.

Harvesting Techniques and Tips

- Harvest pawpaws in early fall.
- Ripe ones will feel soft and have a fruity aroma.
- They are light green or yellow, while unripe ones are green.
- Ripe pawpaws don't always change colors, so focus on the smell and touch.
- Harvest by holding the fruit and twisting.
- You can also shake the branch, and ripe pawpaws will fall to the ground, ready for you to collect.
- Pawpaws are delicate and susceptible to bruising, so be gentle when picking them, or they will bruise.

Nuts

Hickory Nuts: They grow all over the Midwest, especially in southeastern Nebraska and southeastern Minnesota.

Harvesting Techniques and Tips

- Harvest hickory nuts in early fall.
- The nuts husk should be gray/brown, and the shell interior should be brown. They will be easily plucked.
- Ripe nuts fall from trees, so you can collect them from the ground.
- Avoid cracked, discolored, or blemished nuts or ones with rotten spots.

Seeds

Milkweed Seeds: These are native to Missouri and available in many states in the Midwest region.

Harvesting Techniques and Tips

- Harvest milkweed seeds in mid or late fall.
- Ripe seeds are brown and open easily with a gentle press or squeeze, while unripe seeds are pale, cream, light brown, green, or white.
- Ripe seed pods are golden brown.
- Milkweed seeds don't ripen at the same time.
- Harvest the seeds before the pods split.

- Harvest by plucking off the pod, opening it, and pulling out the seeds with your fingers.

Sunflower Seeds: The Midwest has been home to sunflowers for over 2000 years. They grow in the wild and in gardens.

Harvesting Techniques and Tips

- Harvest sunflower seeds in mid-fall.

- Harvest when the seeds turn black, the plant's back and leaves turn yellow, the flowers dry out, and the head drops.

- Ripe seeds are loose and plump.

- Cut the stems about an inch below the head using pruners or sharp scissors.

- Remove the seeds by rubbing the flower's head with your hands over a basket or a large bowl to catch the seeds.

- Before using the seeds, remove the petals and other parts of the flower that fell into the container.

Berries

Ripe elderberries are black or dark purple, juicy, and soft.[18]

Elderberries: These are native to the Midwest and grow in all its states, especially Missouri.

Harvesting Techniques and Tips

- Harvest elderberries in early fall.
- Ripe elderberries are black or dark purple, juicy, and soft.
- Unripe elderberries are pale purple or green.
- Harvest by cutting the whole cluster below the base with sharp scissors and removing the berries.

Blackberries: These grow in most of the Midwest states, especially in south Illinois and Missouri.

Harvesting Techniques and Tips

- Harvest wild blackberries in early fall.
- Pick ripe blackberries by hand.
- Don't pick wet berries because they can squish or mold.
- Blackberry harvesting season lasts three weeks, so pick the berries twice a week.
- Harvest blackberries early in the morning or at dusk to avoid the heat.
- Wear pants, long-sleeved shirts, and hiking shoes to protect yourself from the thorns.
- Ripe berries are dark-colored and firm.
- Wash and eat them right after harvesting, or store them in the fridge, as they won't last more than a day if it isn't refrigerated.

The Significance of Sustainable Harvesting

Sustainable harvesting protects the ecosystem by harvesting natural resources using ethical methods to reduce the negative impact on the environment. For instance, when harvesting ramps, cut one leaf and leave the second one and the bulb to continue growing. You create balance as you allow for more ramps to grow and make up for the ones you took. This method ensures that natural resources remain intact to provide for present and future generations.

Sustainable harvesting promotes regeneration by freeing space for new plants and trees to grow. It preserves natural resources to create a stable and secure food system for humans and animals.

Practice sustainable harvesting by only taking what you need and avoiding wasting natural resources. For instance, you should only harvest ripe fruits so the tree continues reproducing more fruits. Picking unripe ones is a waste since you will neither use them nor give them a chance to grow.

You should know the life cycles of wild plants, the characteristics of ripe ones, and the best time for harvest. You also shouldn't waste any parts of the harvested plants. Instead of discarding them, cook them, use them as garnish, or dry them and use them as herbs.

Sustainable harvesting also protects the climate by reducing habitat destruction and deforestation, which contribute to releasing carbon dioxide, trapping heat, and raising the Earth's temperature.

Take what you want and discard the rest. Some people don't care about future generations and focus only on themselves. However, the future is coming sooner than you think! Scientists have warned against climate change and its impact on the planet for years. They said there was still time for people to change their ways and protect the environment. Unfortunately, only a few people listened, while others dismissed these claims or thought climate change wouldn't happen in the 21st century. They were wrong.

Now, many have seen the impact of human activities on the environment, and no one can ignore it anymore. Practice sustainable harvesting for a better future for yourself and your loved ones.

Winter

It is the last month of the year when nature goes into a deep slumber. In cold weather, respiration and photosynthesis slow down, leading some plants to die while others stop growing. However, some plants are resilient and can survive and thrive in cold weather and under ice and snow.

Plants

Wintercress: It grows throughout the Midwest, except for North Dakota.

Harvesting Techniques and Tips

- Harvest wintercress in late winter.
- Harvest the leaves when they look green and fresh.

Chickweed grows in all states in the Midwest, especially Illinois, where it is found in every county.

Harvesting Techniques and Tips

- Harvest chickweed in mid or late winter.

- Cut off a couple of inches from the top, rinse, and store in the refrigerator.

- Harvest when the plant looks supple and fresh.

Fungi

Mushroom Oysters: They are common in Illinois and grow on decaying trees, stumps, fallen logs, or rotten wood.

Harvesting Techniques and Tips

- Harvest oyster mushrooms anytime during the year.

- Pick them when they are still young. Older mushrooms have a strange flavor.

The four seasons paint Earth with different colors every few months. This allows different plants to grow, flourish, and provide resources for all living creatures. Nature never stops giving. Even during the cold, strong plants can still survive and bloom.

People must give back to nature and protect it by practicing sustainable harvesting. If you take a leaf, ensure another will grow in its place.

Chapter 4: Wild Edible Plants of the Midwest

Whether it's lush forests, fertile farmlands, or an oasis in a desert, plants have sustained humans and wildlife for centuries. Throughout this chapter, you'll explore recognizable and safe-to-consume wild edible plants native to the Midwest. From the delicate flavors of woodland herbs to the hearty nourishment of wild roots and tubers, you'll uncover the characteristics, habitats, benefits, and uses of these botanical wonders. Each plant listed here will connect you more to the land.

Greens and Shoots

Dandelion *(Taraxacum officinale)*

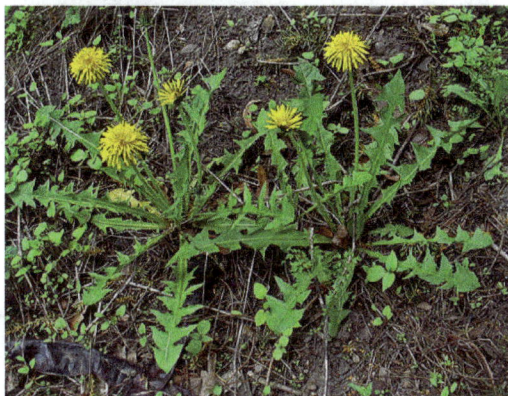

Dandelion leaves are short, deeply toothed, and form a flower-like pattern around their bright yellow flowers.[a]

- **Characteristics:** Dandelion leaves are long and narrow, with large backward-facing "teeth", and grow directly from the ground in a circular *rosette*. The bright yellow "flowers" – technically compound inflorescences with 50-100 individual *florets* – emerge from the centers of these rosettes, on hollow, leafless stalks called *scapes*. The flowers ripen into fluffy seed heads, which disperse quickly in the wind.

- **Habitat:** Dandelions thrive in fertile, disturbed soils, but otherwise can be found in almost every imaginable habitat, from lawns and gardens to roadsides and meadows.

- **Season:** Dandelion greens can be harvested whenever you find them, but are most abundant in early spring. Young leaves are tenderer and less bitter than larger and older leaves, and cooking moderates their sharp flavor.

- **Nutritional Benefits:** Dandelion greens have anti-inflammatory effects, reduce cholesterol levels and blood sugar, and may even decrease cancer risks. They are rich in vitamins A, C, and K, calcium, iron, and potassium.

Caution: Dandelions can often be found in habitats where they may be exposed to potentially toxic contaminants like fertilizers, pesticides, and pet waste. Always harvest from wild populations to avoid exposure to these toxins.

Lamb's Quarters *(Chenopodium album)*

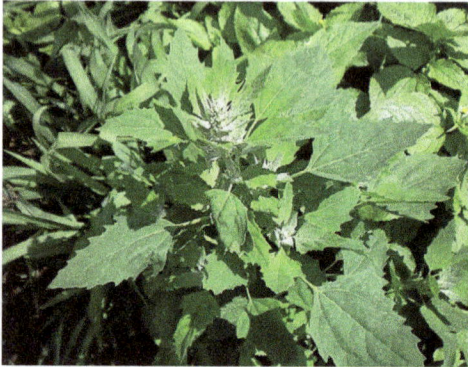

Lamb's quarters have diamond-shaped, toothed leaves covered in a white powdery coating, giving them a frosted appearance.[16]

- **Characteristics:** Goosefoot is a leggy shrub with triangular to diamond-shaped leaves, which are irregularly serrated and frequently have a powdery or "floury" appearance produced by small glands that grow on the leaves. Generally the uppermost, youngest leaves show this the best, and may appear almost white in color (though if you rub the coating off, they're green underneath).

- **Habitat:** Like dandelions, goosefoot was introduced from the Old World, and like dandelions it grows abundantly in open areas (often the same ones). Gardens, parks, vacant lots, and other disturbed habitats are all likely to host this plant.

- **Season:** Goosefoot can be harvested throughout spring and summer, but the leaves become stringy and unpalatable as they grow and age. An annual plant, goosefoot dies soon after seeding in early fall.

- **Nutritional Benefits:** Goosefoot greens are a nutritional powerhouse, containing high levels of vitamins A, C, and K, as well as eight out of nine essential amino acids and omega-3 fatty acids.

Caution: Goosefoot contains both *saponins* and *oxalic acid*, compounds found in numerous other edible plants (e.g., spinach, some nightshades) but known or believed to be toxic in very large quantities. These compounds are degraded by the cooking process, and pose few or no health risks when consumed in moderation, but sensitive persons should avoid raw goosefoot greens.

Sorrel *(Rumex* spp.*)*

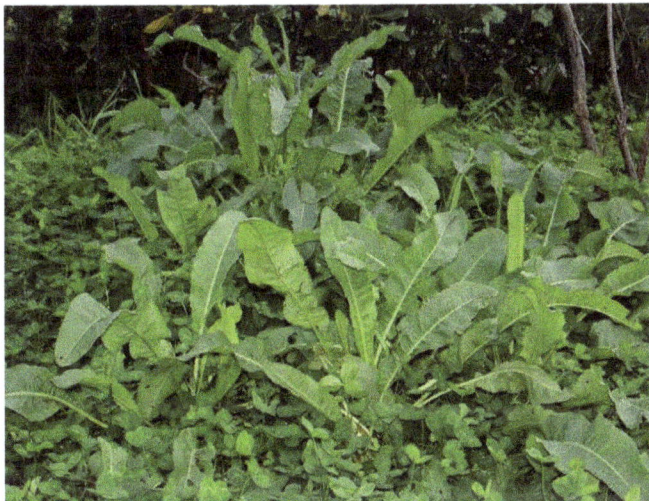

Curly dock (R. crispus), one of the most common species in North America, is easily identified by its "crisped" or wavy-edged leaves, which are similar in appearance and texture (though not in flavor) to mustard greens.[16]

- **Characteristics:** Dock or sorrel has long, relatively narrow lance- or arrow-shaped leaves with long petioles (leaf stalks), often tinged with red at the base like the closely related rhubarb (*Rheum* x *hybridus*). The leaves emerge in very early spring and form a loose rosette, followed by a tall flowering stalktopped with small clusters of inconspicuous green or reddish flowers. In late summer, these mature into small seeds enclosed in papery husks.

- **Habitat:** Sorrel prefers moist soils, and can be found along the margins of ponds and streams, roadside ditches, and other low-lying areas where water regularly flows or collects.

- **Season:** Sorrel leaves are best harvested in spring, when they are young and tender. Older leaves are stringier and often unpleasantly sour.

- **Nutritional Benefits:** The plant is loaded with fiber, vitamins A, C, potassium, and antioxidants.

Caution: Dock, to an even greater extent than goosefoot, is high in oxalic acid, which is responsible for both its distinctive tang and rhubarb's – and like rhubarb, dock leaves should be eaten in moderation, particularly fresh leaves (cooking degrades most, though not all, of the oxalic acid present in the leaves).

Plantain *(Plantago major)*

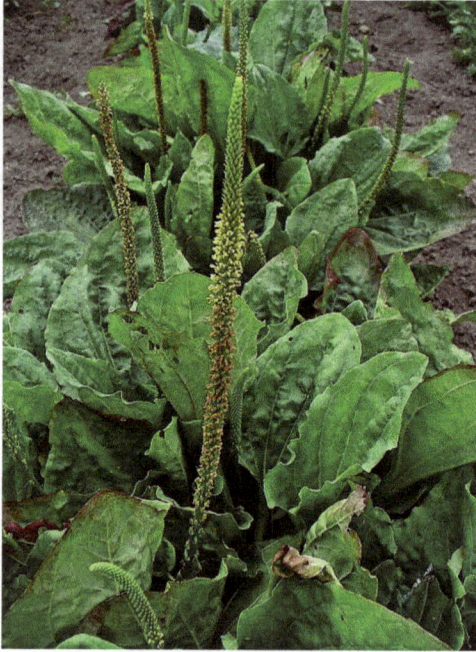

Plantain has broad, oval-shaped leaves with prominent veins, as well as a distinctive spike-like inflorescence.[17]

- **Characteristics:** Plantain leaves are broad and oval-shaped, with long petioles and prominent veins. Its Latin name, *plantago*, means "foot", and refers to the resemblance of the leaf to the human foot. Its flowers, which are tiny and wind-pollinated, emerge on long cylindrical spikes from the center of a rosette.

- **Habitat:** Plantain is well-known for its ability to colonize compacted soils, and is often found growing along hiking trails or roadsides, particularly in moist areas. Stream banks, lawns, and old fields are other places you're likely to see it.

- **Season:** Plantain greens are best when new, from early to mid-spring. The veins become inedibly tough as the leaves age; you can still eat older leaves if you cut the veins out, but they are best cooked.

- **Nutritional Benefits:** All parts of plantain are exceptionally rich in dietary fiber (*psyllium husk* fiber comes from a closely related species), as well as carbohydrates, proteins, potassium, vitamins A, C, B6, and calcium.

Asparagus *(Asparagus officinalis)*

The edible shoots of asparagus will, if left alone, develop into feathery, fern-like foliage with delicate yellow flowers. This plant is definitely too old to harvest![18]

- **Characteristics:** Mature asparagus has feathery, fern-like foliage, borne on long, thin stems up to 6 feet tall. However, it easier to recognize in early spring, when all that is visible of the plant is the young shoots (stems), 12-18 inches in height and studded with embryonic, scale-like leaves.

- **Habitat:** Widely grown as a garden vegetable, asparagus has frequently escaped cultivation over the years and now grows wild along fences, ditches, and roadsides across the country.

- **Season:** Asparagus shoots are harvested just as they emerge in late spring: the younger shoots are more tender and have a superior flavor. If you harvest sparingly from individual plants, you will be able to harvest multiple times in a single season, as well as ensure the persistence of the plants over the years.

- **Nutritional Benefits:** Asparagus has dietary fiber, potassium, vitamin C, B6, and trace amounts of other essential nutrients.

Caution: The young shoots of some legumes can closely resemble asparagus, even to experienced foragers; some of these, like wild indigo (*Baptisia* spp.), are toxic (though not fatally so). The best way to avoid confusion is simply to observe plants in the field before harvesting: by familiarizing yourself with a plant's appearance at *all* life stages, you dramatically reduce the risk of confusing it with a common (or not-so-common) lookalike.

Chickweed *(Stellaria media)*

Chickweed is identified by its small but distinctive white flowers, which have five deeply notched petals – as well as by its trailing stems, which have a distictive line of hairs down one side.[19]

- **Characteristics:** Chickweed is best identified by its overall growth habit: prostrate, with trailing stems and diminutive leaves arranged in opposed pairs. Look closer, and you'll see that each stem is slightly square (like a mint plant), ad has a single line of hairs running along one side of the stem. (This line of hairs is unique to the species and helpful in distinguishing it from similar plants.) The flowers, which last only a few weeks, have five white petals, which are so deeply notched as to appear doubled (from eye level, they look a little like tiny daisies).

- **Habitat:** Chickweed thrives in moist, disturbed areas: stream banks and forest edges, but also roadsides, vacant lots, and even your backyard (it particularly likes growing underneath leaky spigots).

- **Season:** Chickweed can be harvested year-round in mild climates, but as a winter annual it is most abundant in early spring, with a brief "second harvest" from early autumn to the first frost.

- **Nutritional Benefits:** Chickweed greens contain vitamins A, B complex, C, potassium, Copper, zinc, magnesium, and omega-6 fatty acids.

Caution: Numerous inconspicuous annuals may be mistaken for chickweed, from the harmless speedwell (*Veronica* spp.) to the toxic scarlet pimpernel (*Anagallis arvensis*). To avoid confusion, always confirm that your plants have four-angled stems, with a single line of hairs running along one side – no similar plants, edible or toxic, have this trait.

Nettles (Urtica dioica)

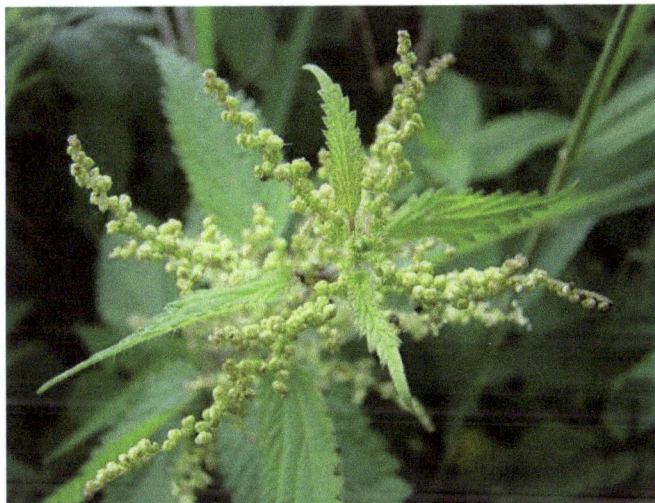

Nettles have serrated, heart-shaped leaves and produce small, greenish flower clusters.[20]

- **Characteristics:** Nettles are tall, slender herbs that can reach six feet or more in height, with serrated, lance- or heart-shaped leaves. All parts of the plant are covered in stinging hairs that can cause skin irritation upon contact.

- **Habitat:** Nettles grow in sunny, damp, nutrient-rich soils, especially along stream banks and in boggy or low-lying open areas.

- **Season:** Nettle greens should be harvested in early spring, ideally before they reach hip height, as the leaves of older plants are tough and stringy.

- **Nutritional Benefits:** Nettle greens contain proteins, calcium, Iron, Magnesium, and essential vitamins.

Caution: Wear gloves when handling nettles to avoid skin irritation from their stinging hairs. Cook or dry nettles before consuming to avoid getting stung.

Purslane *(Portulaca oleracea)*

- **Characteristics:** Purslane has smooth, succulent leaves and produces small yellow flowers. It grows close to the ground in spreading mats.

- **Habitat:** Sunny, dry locations, including gardens, cultivated fields, and disturbed soils, are the best places to find Purslane.

- **Season:** It's harvested in summer when it is at its peak growth.
- **Nutritional Benefits:** Purslane contains vitamin C, B6, calcium, potassium, and proteins.

Caution: Avoid harvesting Purslane from areas treated with herbicides or pesticides, and avoid confusing it with toxic look-alikes like spurge *(Euphorbia spp.)*.

Wild Garlic *(Allium vineale)*

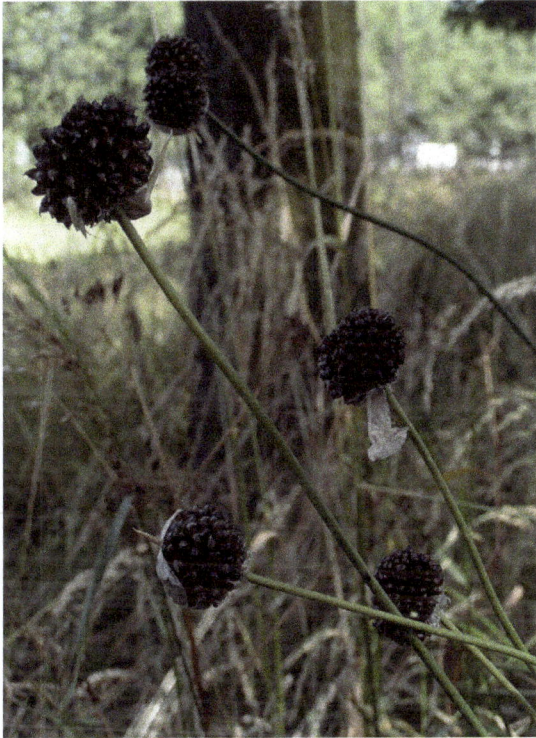

Wild garlic has slender leaves that give off a strong garlic odor when crushed.[11]

- **Characteristics:** True to its name, wild garlic is a close relative of true garlic, onions, and chives – they're all members of the genus *Allium*. It's easily identified by its very long and narrow leaves, which may reach up to two feet long but are rarely more than a few millimeters wide. The leaves, which arise from leek-like bulbs, tend to roll inwards, forming hollow tubes that clasp the base of the flowering stalk or *scape*, which blooms in mid- to late summer. Each scape bears up to 50 tiny, six-petaled pink flowers – though some plants produce *bulbils*, clonal bulbs about the size of a pea, instead of flowers.

- **Habitat:** Wild garlic grows in sunny, fertile soils, particularly along stream banks and in old agricultural fields.

- **Season:** The leaves, young and tender in spring, tend to dry out as the season wears on. The bulbs, contrarily, are best harvested in the autumn, while the bulbils (which taste similar to the bulbs) can be gathered throughout the summer.

- **Nutritional Benefits:** Wild garlic is rich in vitamins A and C, calcium, copper, iron, and sulfur compounds with potential health benefits.

Caution: Many plants have leaves that are vaguely similar to wild garlic's, including nearly a hundred other species of *Allium*, most of which are edible – but also toxic plants like crowpoison (*Nothoscordum bivalve*) and the death camas (*Toxicoscordion* spp.). While it may not always be possible to distinguish wild garlic from a close relative, *only* edible species smell like onions or garlic, which can help distinguish them from potentially dangerous lookalikes.

Wood Sorrel *(Oxalis spp.)*

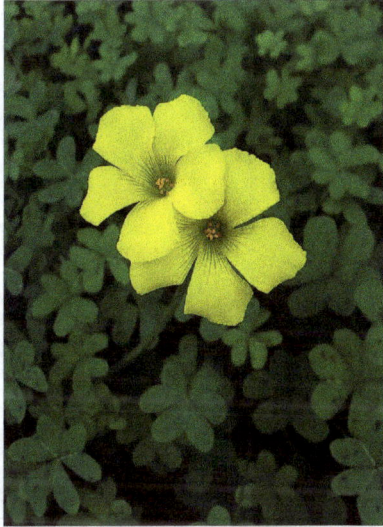

The plant's leaves are divided into three leaflets, with delicate white or yellow flowers.[25]

- **Characteristics:** Though not closely related to true sorrel (see "Dock"), woodsorrel's shamrock-like leaves do taste similar, due to the presence of oxalic acid. The leaves grow from the weakly trailing stems on very long petioles, and are divided into three heart-shaped leaflets; the flowers, though small, are quite pretty, with five backward-curving petals that are generally yellow or white in color (occasionally purple).

- **Habitat:** Woodsorrel, true to its name, often grows in woodland areas, though some species prefer open or disturbed habitats. Woodland edges, bottomland forests, and even backyards and gardens are often rife with woodsorrel in both spring and fall.

- **Season:** Native woodsorrel emerges and blooms in spring, while the introduced violet woodsorrel (*O. violacea*) blooms in summer and autumn. The leaves can be harvested any time, and the green seed pods can also be eaten, with a similar flavor.

- **Nutritional Benefits:** Wood sorrel is high in vitamins A, C, iron, magnesium, and manganese.

Caution: Wood sorrel is generally safe to consume, but it contains high levels of oxalic acid (which is named for its genus). It is harmless when eaten in moderation, but avoid eating it in large quantities or over a prolonged period.

Wild Mustard Greens *(Brassica* spp.*)*

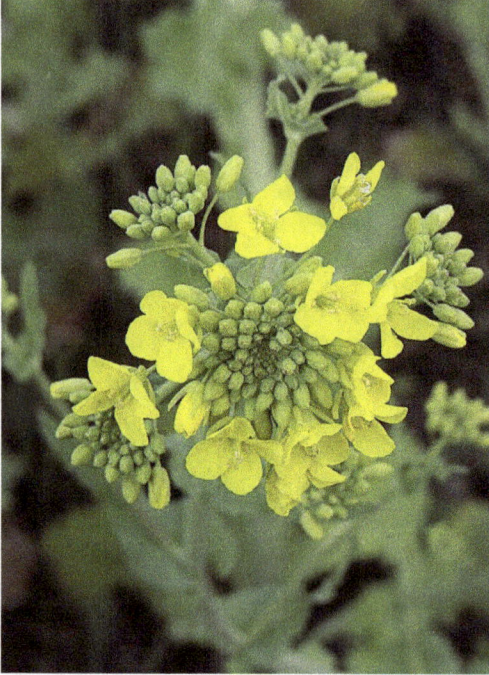

Wild mustard produces clusters of yellow flowers resembling cultivated mustard plants.[33]

- **Characteristics:** Wild mustard has lobed, often lyrate (resembling a violin or guitar) leaves and a pungent, spicy flavor. It produces clusters of yellow flowers with four petals in an X or cross shape.

- **Habitat:** Wild mustard grows abundantly in fields, roadsides, and waste areas.

- **Season:** The greens can be harvested throughout the growing season, but the leaves are most tender in spring.

- **Nutritional Benefits:** Wild mustard greens have vitamins A, B1, B2, C, and antioxidants.

Note: Numerous species of *Brassica* resemble one another quite closely, but all plants in its family (Brassicaceae) are safe to eat. Always look for the yellow, cross-shaped flowers when starting out, to ensure proper identification.

Edible Flowers

Violets *(Viola spp.)*

Violets have heart-shaped leaves and delicate, five-petaled flowers ranging from purple to white.[14]

- **Characteristics:** Violets have heart-shaped leaves and delicate, five-petaled flowers ranging from purple to white.

- **Habitat:** Woodlands, meadows, and gardens are natural habitats of violet growth.

- **Season:** These beautiful flowers bloom in spring and can be harvested throughout the growing season.

- **Edible Uses:** Violet flowers have a mild, slightly sweet flavor and can be used fresh in salads, desserts, or garnish.

Elderflowers *(Sambucus spp.)*

Elderflowers are clusters of small, creamy white flowers with a sweet, floral aroma.[15]

- **Characteristics:** The elder tree – really more of a large shrub – is native to both North America and Europe, and has been used for food and medicine for centuries on both continents. The tree has distinctive leaves, which are both compound (each leaf comprises 5 or 7 small leaflets) and opposite (arranged in pairs on the stem). The flowers emerge in mid-spring, often in great profusion; the flat-topped white clusters can be seen – and smelled – from a great distance. While the flowers fade by early summer, the berries (discussed below) are also edible, though with some caveats.

- **Habitat:** Elders grow at the margins of woodlands and along roadsides and streambanks. They are particularly abundant on disturbed soils, and can form large clonal colonies of numerous individual trees that are connected belowground.

- **Season:** Elderflowers bloom in late spring and early summer, and the flowers must be harvested and processed as soon as possible to ensure freshness. In France, great care is taken when harvesting elderflowers to avoid crushing or bruising the petals.

- **Edible Uses:** Elderflowers can be steeped to make a healthy, caffeine-free tea, or made into syrups, cordials, and even wine.

Rose Petals *(Rosa spp.)*

Rose petals are fragrant and come in various colors, including red, pink, white, and yellow.[36]

- **Characteristics:** Rose petals are fragrant and come in a variety of colors, including red, pink, white, and yellow.

- **Habitat:** These flowering plants are mostly found in gardens and landscaped areas.

- **Season:** Roses bloom from late spring to early summer, depending on the variety.

- **Edible Uses:** The sweet and floral flavor is used in desserts, syrups, jams, and beverages. They can also be crystallized or used fresh as a garnish.

Clovers *(Trifolium* spp.*)*

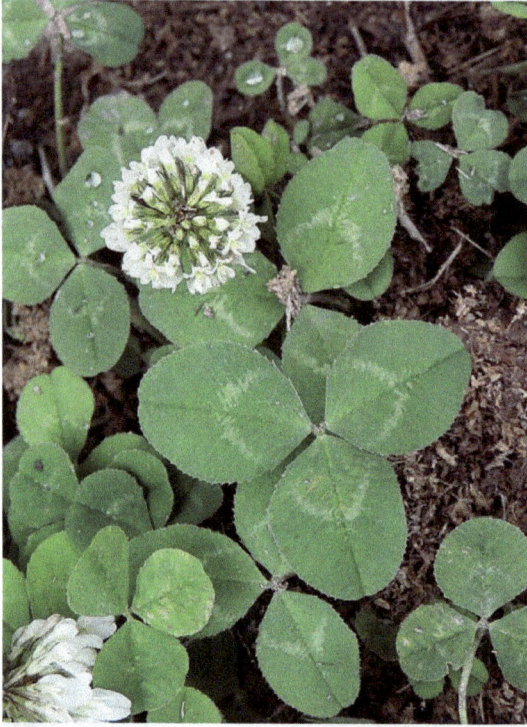

Clover flowers are small, white, or pink, with distinctive three-lobed leaves.[37]

- **Characteristics:** Clover's compound leaves are probably their most famous trait, but they're hardly distinctive. On the other hand, their globe-like flower clusters are both eye-catching and unique: they look like tiny fireworks, comprising a few dozen small white or pink flowers, and are generally the tallest thing on this plant, which has a trailing or creeping habit.

- **Habitat:** The two most common species, red (*T. pratense*) and white clover (*T. repens*), are widespread in lawns, fields, and meadows across the country. They thrive on disturbed ground, and their ability to use atmospheric nitrogen allows them to thrive in infertile soils, making them common early-successional species.

- **Season:** Clovers bloom from spring to early summer.

- **Edible Uses:** Both the leaves and flowers of clover have a mild, slightly sweet flavor. They can be added fresh to salads or desserts, cooked as a potherb, or steeped into a fragrant tea.

Daylilies (*Hemerocallis* spp.)

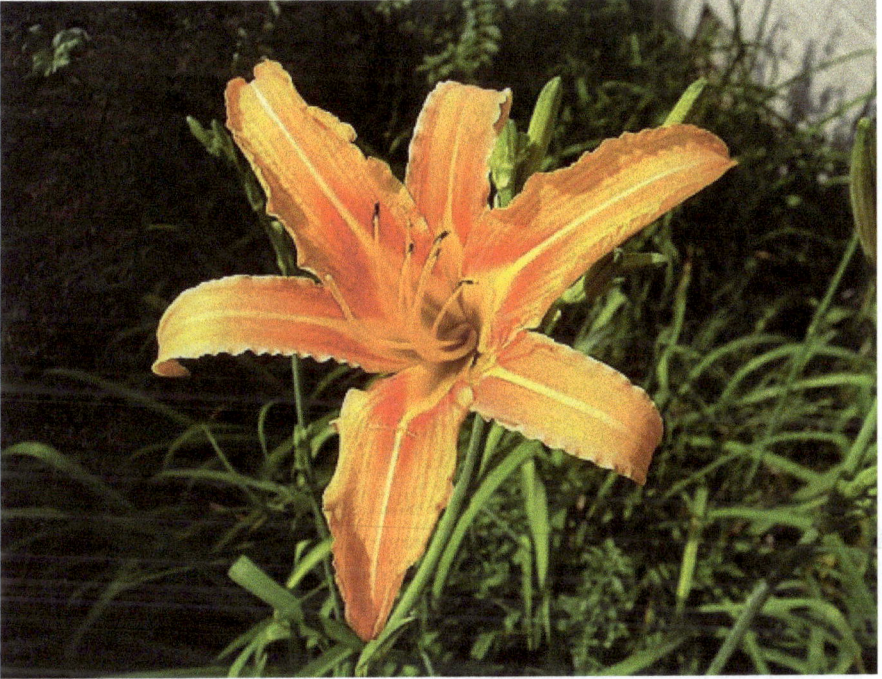

Daylily flowers have six petals and come in various colors, including yellow, orange, and red.[38]

- **Characteristics:** Daylilies are relatives of true lilies (*Lilium* spp.), and their flowers are similar in color and appearance. However, daylily flowers are smaller and emerge in clusters rather than singly, and – true to their name – last only a day or so before fading and dropping off.

- **Habitat:** Originally a cultivated garden and landscape plant, it has naturalized throughout the eastern United States, where it can be found growing in wet meadows and pastures, along creek and river banks, and in open woodlands.

- **Season:** Daylilies bloom in summer, and although individual flowers are short-lived, many plants will bloom multiple times in a single season – so don't feel too bad if you miss the first flush!

- **Edible Uses:** Daylily flowers have a dense, nearly meaty texture and slightly sweet flavor; fresh, they are excellent in salads, as well as added to stir-fries and soups just before serving.

Bee Balm *(Monarda* spp.*)*

Wild bergamot (M. fistulosa) is one of the most common species of bee balm; other species bloom in shades of red, pink, or white, but all share the distinctive tubular shape and whisker-like stamens.[29]

- **Characteristics:** Also known as wild bergamot, bee balm does indeed bear a certain olfactory resemblance to bergamot (which isn't closely related). Generally pink or purple, the distinctively spurred and funnel-shaped flowers mark bee balm as a member of the mint family (Lamiaceae), as do the square stem and opposite leaves; however, unlike true mints, bee balm's flowers emerge in circular or globe-like clusters.

- **Habitat:** Bee balm loves full sun, and can be found in meadows and pastures, along stream banks, and in woodland clearings and edges.

- **Season:** While the exact timing depends on the species, most bee balms bloom throughout summer, setting seed soon afterward. The flowers should be harvested when at their most vibrant and aromatic, then dried in a dehydrator (or air-dried in the shade) to prevent the loss of the aromatic compounds responsible for their unique smell and flavor.

- **Edible Uses:** Fresh flowers can be added to salads, while dried flowers can be steeped into tea, either alone or mixed with black tea. Use in moderation, as a little of the dried flowers goes a long way.

Johnny-Jump-Up *(Viola tricolor)*

These flowers are small and colorful, with purple, yellow, and white petals.[30]

- **Characteristics:** These flowers are small and colorful, with purple, yellow, and white petals.

- **Habitat:** It grows in meadows, fields, and gardens.

- **Season:** The flowers bloom from spring to early summer.

- **Edible Uses:** Johnny-jump-up flowers have a mild, slightly sweet flavor and can be dried or added fresh to desserts and beverages.

Wild Berries

Blueberries *(Vaccinium spp.)*

Blueberries are small, round berries with a dark blue-purple color and a sweet-tart flavor.[31]

- **Characteristics:** Plants in the genus *Vaccinium* are variously known as blueberries, cranberries, huckleberries, bilberries, and farkleberries, depending on who you ask. Several species with small, spherical blue berries are called "blueberries", the most common midwestern species being the lowbush blueberry (*V. angustifolium*). Apart from their distinctive fruits, blueberries can be recognized by their glossy, blue-green leaves – which turn vibrant shades of red and orange in the autumn – and their preference for acidic, mucky soils, which few other plants share.

- **Habitat:** Blueberries grow in a wide range of habitats, from mountain forests to low-lying swamps, but are most common on poor and/or acidic soils. This means they can often be found as early-successional species in disturbed habitats, such as recently burned forests or in the aftermath of landslides and floods.

- **Season:** Blueberries ripen in mid to late summer. If you've found a productive patch, watch it closely and harvest in moderation, as you're probably sharing it with dozens or even hundreds of other critters, large and small, who rely on its bounty!

- **Edible Uses:** There's really no wrong way to eat a blueberry, whether enjoyed straight from the bush or made into pies, turnovers, jams, and jellies.

Raspberries *(Rubus* spp.*)*

Raspberries are small, round berries with various colors, including red, black, purple, and golden.[33]

- **Characteristics:** Raspberries are small, round berries with various colors, including red, black, purple, and golden.

- **Habitat:** These berries are packed with antioxidants and grow in sunny areas in forests, along roadsides, and in open fields.

- **Season:** Raspberries ripen in mid to late summer.

- **Edible Uses:** You can eat fresh or use it in baking, add it to beverages, or process it to make jams and syrups.

Blackberries *(Rubus spp.)*

Blackberries are larger, elongated berries with a dark purple-black color and a sweet-tart flavor.[88]

- **Characteristics:** These are larger, elongated berries with a dark purple-black color and a sweet-tart flavor.

- **Season:** The ripening season is between mid to late summer.

- **Edible Uses:** Eat fresh and dry to preserve them longer, or make delicious treats like jams, pies, and beverages.

Wild Strawberries *(Fragaria* spp.*)*

These sweet berries have a bright red color and an intense flavor.[a]

- **Characteristics:** These sweet berries have a bright red color and an intense flavor.
- **Habitat:** Wild strawberries grow naturally in woodland clearings and edges, and along streambanks and hiking trails.
- **Season:** Fruits emerge and ripen late spring or early summer.
- **Edible Uses:** Enjoy fresh, add to salads, desserts, or used in jams and syrups.

Serviceberries *(Amelanchier arborea)*

Juneberries are also known as serviceberries or Saskatoon berries.[35]

- **Characteristics:** Serviceberry – also called juneberry, shadberry, and Saskatoon berry – is a small tree in the rose family (Rosaceae), with finely serrated leaves that are often slightly heart-shaped at their bases. The flowers, which appear before the leaves, are followed in June by deep red berries about the size and shape of blueberries.

- **Habitat:** Serviceberry grows in a wide range of habitats, but is most common in open woodlands and along woodland edges and stream banks.

- **Season:** Serviceberries ripen in late spring and early summer.

- **Edible Uses:** Make muffins, jams, jellies, and pies, or eat them fresh after foraging.

Gooseberries *(Ribes spp.)*

These are small, round berries with translucent skin and a tart flavor.[36]

- **Characteristics:** These are small, round berries with translucent skin and a tart flavor.

- **Habitat:** Gooseberries grow on shrubs in woodlands, fields, and near streams.

- **Season:** From mid to late summer, gooseberries can be foraged.

- **Edible Uses:** Gooseberries are used in pies, tarts, jams, and preserves or enjoyed fresh if fully ripe.

Chokeberries *(Aronia spp.)*

Chokeberries, or Aronia berries, are small, round berries with a dark purple-black color and a tart flavor.[87]

- **Characteristics:** Chokeberries, or Aronia berries, are small, round berries with a dark purple-black color and a tart flavor.

- **Habitat:** Chokeberries grow on shrubs in wetlands, hilly fields, and near flowing water sources.

- **Season:** Chokeberries are safe to consume in late summer to early fall.

- **Edible Uses:** Eat them when fully ripe, or add the ingredients to your desserts for a refreshing taste.

Huckleberry *(Gaylussacia baccata)*

Huckleberries are small, round berries with a dark blue-purple color and a sweet-tart flavor.[58]

- **Characteristics:** Huckleberry is low, many-stemmed shrub similar in appearance to its close relatives, blueberries and cranberries (*Vaccinium* spp.). Its leaves are lance-shaped and slightly glossy, and the undersides are dotted with resin glands that help distinguish the species from blueberries and cranberries.

- **Habitat:** Like its relatives, huckleberry thrives on moist, acidic soils, and is commonly found in bogs and swamps, as well as in the understory of open woodlands, particularly pine and oak forests.

- **Season:** You can forage them mid to late summer when the berries are fully ripe.

- **Edible Uses:** Huckleberries can be eaten raw or cooked in any context where you might use blueberries. They're an excellent addition to any diet due to their high antioxidant content and vitamins.

Red Mulberries *(Morus rubra)*

These oblong berries have a deep red to dark purple color and a sweet flavor when ripe.[89]

- **Characteristics:** Red mulberry is a small, shrubby tree easily recognized by its distinctive leaves, which are broadly heart-shaped but often develop irregular lobes as they develop. The berries – multiple fruits that superficially resemble blackberries (though they're more closely related to figs) – turn from pale green to deep purple-black as they ripen.

- **Habitat:** Red mulberry grows in a range of habitats including open woods, stream banks, and pastures. They're particularly particularly common along fence lines, where their seeds are often spread by songbirds.

- **Season:** Their ripening period is from late spring to early summer.

- **Edible Uses:** Mulberries can be eaten fresh, but processing them (into pies, jams, syrups, etc.) concentrates and improves their flavor.

Wild Plums *(Prunus americana)*

With a sweet-tart flavor, wild plums produce round fruits with reddish-purple skin.[40]

- **Characteristics:** Wild plums are shrubs or small trees with smooth, glossy bark and serrated leaves. Their white flowers emerge in early spring before the leaves, and are typical of many plants in the rose family (Rosaceae): five large petals surrounding a "pincushion" of yellow-tipped stamens. The fruits are glossy and dark red when ripe, often with a "fogged" or "frosted" appearance.

- **Habitat:** Wild plums thrive in disturbed areas with moist soils, including stream banks, roadsides, and the margins of woodlands.

- **Season:** Although they are among the earliest-blooming trees in spring, the fruits generally do not ripen until the end of summer or early fall.

- **Edible Uses:** Delicious fresh, wild plums can also be used in desserts just like grocery store plums, or made into jellies, jams, and even wine.

Nuts and Seeds

Acorns *(Quercus spp.)*

These oval nuts have a hard shell and a cap covering part of the nut."

- **Characteristics:** Acorns are almost instantly recognizable to most people, but far fewer know that they're also edible and nutritious. The best-tasting and "sweetest" acorns generally come from "white" oaks (*Quercus* sect. *Quercus*), while the acorns of "red" oaks (sect. *Lobatae*) contain high levels of bitter tannins. White oaks can be identified by their leaves, which have wavy or smoothly lobed margins; red oak leaves have more jagged or "toothed" appearance.

- **Habitat:** Oaks are ubiquitous throughout the Midwest (and eastern North America in general), and can be found in nearly every habitat. White oak (*Q. alba*), bur oak (*Q. macrocarpa*), and chinkapin oak (*Q. muehlenbergii*) are among most common species with "sweet" acorns.

- **Edible Uses:** Acorns, even those with low tannin levels, must be leached to remove the tannins, either by boiling in two (or more) changes of water or sprouting in wet sand. Once leached, they can be roasted and eaten like chestnuts, or ground into a protein-rich (but gluten-free) flour.

Hickory Nuts *(Carya spp.)*

Hickory nuts are round nuts with a hard shell and a rich, sweet flavor.[48]

- **Characteristics:** Hickory trees are close relatives of pecans (*C. illinoiensis*) and similar in appearance, with flaky gray bark and compound leaves, generally with 5 or 7 leaflets. The round nuts, which resemble walnuts, have hard shells and are enclosed in thick green husks, which split open at maturity.

- **Habitat:** Hickory trees thrive in deep soil, and are most common along rivers and creeks.

- **Edible Uses:** The nuts can be cracked open and eaten raw, roasted, or used in baking. The roasted nuts can also be blended with water to make a Natve American beverage similar to almond milk.

Hazelnuts *(Corylus* spp.*)*

Hazelnuts are round, with a thin, papery husk.[48]

- **Characteristics:** Two species of edible hazelnut can be found in the Midwest: the American hazel (*C. americana*) and the beaked hazel (*C. cornuta*). Both are small trees or shrubs with smooth gray bark and alternate leaves, which have toothed margins and prominent veins. Both species enclose their nuts in odd-looking bracts: those of American hazelnuts are elaborately frilled, while beaked hazelnuts have bracts that form a long, beak-like tube. When these bracts begin to dry out and turn brown, the nuts within are ready to harvest!

- **Habitat:** Both species are common in open woods and along stream banks, fencerows, and roadsides.

- **Edible Uses:** Although smaller than commercial hazelnuts, many foragers consider native hazelnuts have a superior flavor, and they can be eaten raw or roasted just like their larger cousins. Hazelnuts pair well with chocolate, making them a common ingredient in confections, spreads, and desserts.

Beech Nuts *(Fagus grandifolia)*

Beech nuts are triangular nuts cased in a spiny husk."

- **Characteristics:** Beech trees are large and conspicuous trees, with smooth gray bark and distinctively "scalloped" leaves. The fruits, or burs, are easy to recognize – particularly as mature trees can produce tens of thousands in a season. About the size of a gumball, they're covered with curving spines, which (fortunately) split open as they dry to release the triangular "beech nuts".

- **Habitat:** Beeches are common throughout eastern North America, especially in old-growth forests, and often alongside sugar maple (*Acer saccharinum*). Beech trees found in urban areas are mostly European beeches (*F. sylvatica*), whose seeds are also edible but can be mildly toxic if eaten in large quantities.

- **Edible Uses:** Raw beech nuts can be bitter due to tannins in the seed coat, but roasting removes the bitter flavor. The seeds themselves are sweet and mild, and can be eaten alone or processed into "beech nut butter".

Pecans *(Carya illinoinensis)*

Pecans have a thin, smooth shell and a distinct buttery flavor."

- **Characteristics:** Pecans are large, spreading trees with compound leaves, each with 9 or 11 (sometimes 13) leaflets. The nut has a thin, smooth shell and is enclosed in a green husk, which turns black and splits along four seams as the nut ripens.

- **Habitat:** Pecan trees grow largest and most abundantly in the deep, fertile soils of river valleys and floodplains, and are commonly used in yards, parks, and urban landscapes.

- **Edible Uses:** Pecans can be eaten raw, roasted, or cooked in desserts, particularly pecan pie.

Black Walnut (*Juglans nigra*)

Black walnuts are encased in thick husks, which turn black and decompose naturally as the nuts within ripen."

- **Characteristics:** Black walnuts are smaller than cultivated walnuts (*J. regia*) and are encased in thick husks, which are green initially and turn black as the fruits ripen. The trees can be identified by their long compound leaves, which have 13-21 leaflets and have a distinctive pungent scent when rubbed or crushed.

- **Habitat:** Black walnut is a common mid-story component of deciduous forests and woodlands, particularly near streams and rivers.

- **Edible Uses:** Black walnuts are often described as sweeter and more flavorful than common walnuts, and can be used similarly in recipes.

Roots and Tubers

Ramps *(Allium tricoccum)*

Wild leeks are easily identified by their leaves, which emerge in early spring; they resemble grass or lily leaves, but much wider, with reddish bases and petioles."

- **Characteristics:** wild leeks, also called ramps, are a prized early-spring delicacy, related to garlic (*Allium sativum*) and onions. The plant is easy to recognize by its broad, lance-shaped leaves, which have reddish bases and emit a distinctive onion-like aroma when crushed. The plants usually die back to the ground by early summer.

- **Habitat:** Wild leeks are found primarily in forests and woodlands, especially in deep, fertile soils along streams and rivers.

- **Edible Uses:** Both the bulbs and leaves of wild leeks are edible, and can be eaten raw, fried, stewed, and even pickled.

Wild Carrots *(Daucus carota)*

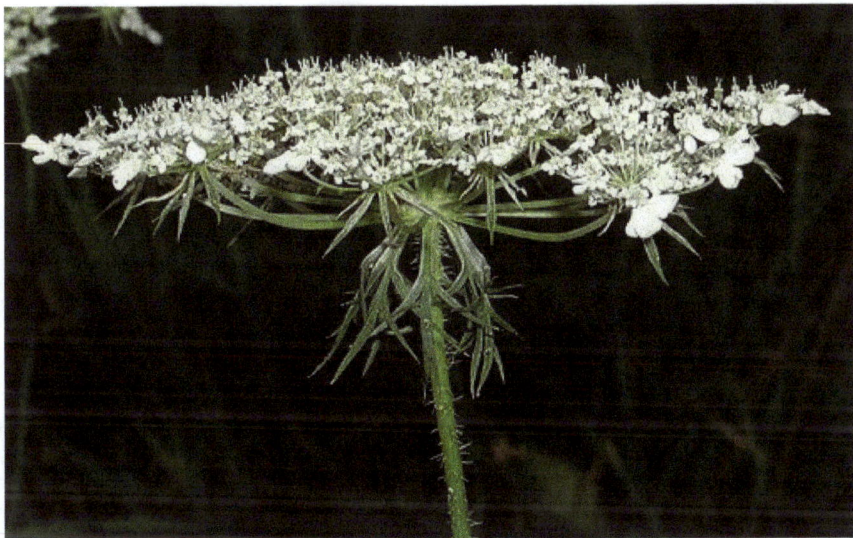

Wild carrots are biennial plants with feathery foliage and white, lacy flowers.*

- **Characteristics:** Wild carrot, also called Queen Anne's lace is a biennial plant native to Europe, now a common weed throughout North America. It is easily recognized by its feathery, compound foliage and white flowers, which form basket-like clusters atop stalks up to 5 feet high. Beware of poison hemlock (*Conium maculatum*), a toxic lookalike occasionally found in similar habitats: it can be distinguished by its red-tinged stems and by its flower clusters, which are round-topped rather than basket-like.

- **Habitat:** Wild carrots thrive in sunny, disturbed soils, particularly near human habitation: pastures, agricultural fields, roadsides, and even vacant lots are all common habitats. It tends to inhabit drier soils than poison hemlock, but their habitats can occasionally overlap, so always confirm your identification before harvesting.

- **Edible Uses:** The taproot is edible when harvested prior to flowering; though it lacks the bright orange color of domestic carrots, it has a similar mild and sweet flavor, and can be eaten raw or cooked.

Wild Radishes *(Raphanus raphanistrum)*

Wild radishes are annual or biennial plants with pungent, peppery roots and white to purple flowers.[49]

- **Characteristics:** Wild radish is an annual plant with lance-shaped leaves, widest near the tip and with irregular lobes closer to the base. These form a basal rosette, from which the flowering stalk or scape emerges in May or June, topped with cross-shaped yellow or white flowers typical of plants in the cabbage family (Brassicaceae). The plant closely resembles wild mustard (*Brassica* spp.), but can be distinguished by its singular flowers (mustard flowers come in clusters).

- **Habitat:** Like many annual plants, wild radishes thrive in disturbed habitats like roadsides, pastures, and even vacant lots.

- **Edible Uses:** All parts of wild radish are edible, with a pungent, peppery flavor. Young greens can be used fresh in salads like arugula, while older leaves can be cooked like mustard greens. The roots of younger plants (before flowering) can be peeled and boiled or roasted, and are have a much milder flavor than supermarket radishes.

Parsnip *(Pastinaca sativa)*

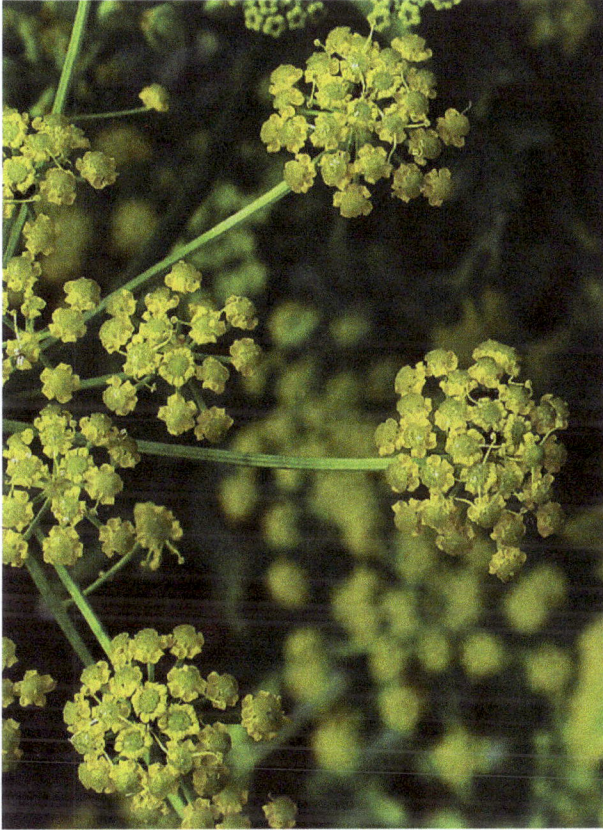

Wild parsnips are biennial plants with tall, hollow stems, compound leaves, and yellow flowers.[50]

- **Characteristics:** Parsnips are biennial plants in the parsley family (Apiaceae), related to carrots (*Daucus carota*) and similar in overall appearance. Parsnip leaves are compound, each leaf consisting of 5-11 serrated and irregularly lobed leaflets; these form a rosette in the first year, followed by a hollow flowering stalk up to 5 feet high and topped with round-topped clusters of yellow flowers.

- **Habitat:** Native to Eurasia, parsnips have naturalized readily throughout the Midwest, and can be found in old fields, roadsides, and other sunny areas.

- **Edible Uses:** Harvest the roots in the first fall or winter, before the plants have flowered. Young roots have a sweet, nutty flavor, and can be used much like carrots.

Sunchokes *(Helianthus tuberosus)*

Wild sunchokes are tall perennial plants with bright yellow flowers and knobby tubers.[51]

- **Characteristics:** Sunchoke, sometimes called Jerusalem artichoke, is a hardy and long-lived sunflower that produces knobby, edible tubers with a taste somewhere between a potato and an artichoke. The plant itself looks a lot like a common sunflower (H. annuus), but can be distinguished by its narrower leaves and smaller flowers with yellow centers.

- **Habitat:** Sunchokes thrive in many of the same habitats as common sunflowers: pastures, roadsides, and native prairies. They bloom in late summer or fall, and the tubers can be harvested any time between fall and spring.

- **Edible Uses:** Sunchokes have a sweet, nutty flavor, and are a good source of iron and potassium. The peeled tubers can be shredded or sliced and eaten raw, or cooked like potatoes – their high sugar content makes them particularly well-suited for roasting.

Field Mustard, Wild Turnip *(Brassica rapa)*

Wild turnips are biennial plants with rosettes of leaves, yellow flowers, and round or elongated roots.[62]

- **Characteristics:** Field mustard is a biennial plant closely related to cabbage and kale (*B. oleracea*), as well as common turnips (*Brassica juncea*). First year plants form rosettes of lyrate (guitar-shaped) leaves similar to kale or turnip greens (though smaller). The following spring, the plants send up long flowering stalks with clasping, teardrop-shaped leaves totally unlike the basal leaves, and topped with a dense cluster of yellow, four-petaled flowers.

- **Habitat:** Field mustard is extraordinarily widely naturalized in North America, and grows abundantly along roadsides, old farm fields, and disturbed areas of all kinds.

- **Edible Uses:** First-year plants have bulbous, white taproots that look like small and have a similarly pungent flavor, which is moderated by cooking. The greens can be harvested at any time, and used just like mustard greens.

Burdocks *(Arctium* spp.*)*

Wild burdock is a biennial plant with large, heart-shaped leaves, purple flowers, and long taproots.[58]

- **Characteristics:** Burdocks are relatives of thistles (*Cirsium* spp.) and artichokes (*Cynara* spp) with large, edible taproots. Flowering burdocks are quite distinctive, reaching six feet high or more, but their roots tend to be tough and unpalatable. Look instead for the large, heart-shaped leaves of first-year plants, which resemble overgrown chard or rhubarb.

- **Habitat:** Originally native to Eurasia, burdocks have naturalized across most of the northern U.S. and Canada, where they are common in meadows and woodland edges, and along roadsides, fencelines, and hiking trails.

- **Edible Uses:** Fresh burdock root has an earthy, slightly sweet flavor and crisp texture somewhat like jicama, while cooked burdock root has a softer texture and sweeter flavor. In Japan, pickled burdock root is popular both as a condiment and sushi ingredient.

Wild Yam *(Dioscorea villosa)*

Now that you know the wild edibles you can find in the Midwest, remember that whatever you forage needs to be inspected thoroughly before you eat it. For example, an unhealthy plant can carry pathogens like bacteria, fungi, and parasites that can affect your health and even result in diseases.

The best approach is to read up more about the plants you want to forage, including watching videos, to identify the flowers, fruits, tubers, and other wild edibles that are safe to consume.

Chapter 5: Mushrooms of the Midwest

Fungi are, most of the time, overlooked but are essential to supporting the web of life within natural ecosystems. They aid in everything from nutrient cycling to the health of plants and animals. Fungi are nature's recyclers, breaking down organic matter like dead trees, leaves, and other debris into simpler compounds. This decomposition process releases carbon, nitrogen, and phosphorus back into the soil, enriching it and sustaining the growth of new plant life. Without fungi, organic material would accumulate, preventing nutrient cycling and deteriorating the ecosystem's health.

Fungi are, most of the time, overlooked but are essential to supporting the web of life within natural ecosystems.[54]

These microscopic fungi form intricate symbiotic relationships with plants, including the famous mycorrhizal associations. Mycorrhizal fungi colonize plant roots, extending their reach into the soil and enhancing their ability to absorb water and nutrients. In return, the fungi receive sugars produced by the plant through photosynthesis. This symbiosis is fundamental for the growth and survival of many plant species, especially in nutrient-poor soils.

While some fungi form beneficial partnerships with plants, others act as natural regulators of plant populations by causing diseases. This might seem counterintuitive, but these fungal pathogens maintain the balance within forest ecosystems by preventing the unchecked spread of certain plant species. They keep the habitat biodiverse by preventing any single species from dominating and outcompeting others.

Several organisms rely on these fungi as their main food source. Many creatures, from insects to small mammals, depend directly or indirectly on fungi for their nutrition. They also support the growth of certain plants that are vital for the diets of herbivores, thereby influencing the entire food web.

Fungi also create and maintain soil structure. Their hyphal networks act as a binding agent, holding soil particles together and preventing erosion. This stabilizes the soil, making life in terrestrial and aquatic ecosystems downstream possible.

Certain fungi are valuable indicators of ecosystem health because they are sensitive to environmental changes. Monitoring their presence and abundance indicates broader ecological trends, including pollution levels, climate change impacts, and habitat degradation. Now that you know fungi's impact on the ecosystem, here is a basic overview of the structures that make up a mushroom.

Mushroom Anatomy

Understanding basic mushroom anatomy and terminology is crucial for accurate identification, especially when foraging for wild mushrooms. Here's a breakdown to lay a solid foundation:

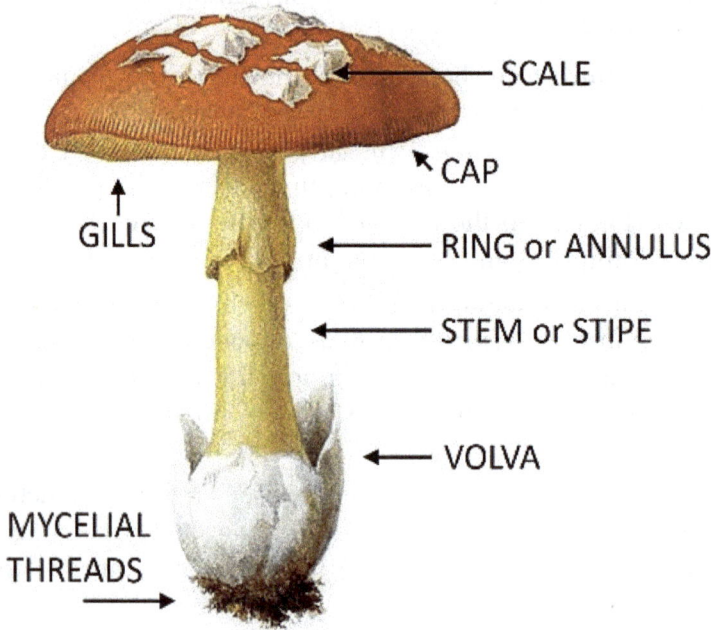

Understanding basic mushroom anatomy and terminology is crucial for accurate identification, especially when foraging for wild mushrooms.[55]

Cap

The cap is the upper part of the mushroom, which is rounded or dome-shaped. Depending on the species, it can vary in size, shape, color, and texture.

Gills

Gills are thin, blade-like structures found underneath the cap. They radiate from the stem to the edge of the cap and produce spores, which are essential for reproduction. The color, spacing, and attachment of gills can be important identification features.

Stem

The stem, or the stipe, is an elongated structure supporting the cap. It can be cylindrical, bulbous, or tapered and may have various textures, colors, and markings.

Ring or Annulus

Some mushrooms have a ring or annulus encircling the stem, a remnant of the partial veil that once protected the gills. The presence, position, and appearance of the ring are crucial for proper identification.

Volva

A volva is a cup-like structure at the base of some mushrooms. It forms during the early stages of growth and may remain a distinct feature or degrade over time. The presence or absence of a volva is essential for accurate identification, especially in certain toxic species.

Veil

The veil is a membrane-like structure that covers and protects the developing gills in young mushrooms. As the mushroom matures, the veil may rupture, leaving remnants on the cap, stem, or as a ring around the stem.

Spore Print

Spores are microscopic reproductive cells produced by mushrooms. A spore print is created by placing the cap of a mature mushroom on a piece of paper or glass, allowing the spores to drop and form a pattern. The color of the spores is another aspect that aids in identification.

Hyphae

Hyphae are thread-like structures that make up the body of the mushroom. This body or mycelium grows underground or within its substrate, absorbing nutrients and breaking down organic matter.

Accurate identification is critical when foraging wild mushrooms because of the potential risks of consuming toxic species. Some mushrooms closely resemble edible varieties but can be deadly if ingested. Therefore, always rely on multiple identification features, including cap, gill structure, spore print, and habitat, and cross-reference with reliable field guides or expert mycologists to be on the safe side.

Always be careful when foraging wild mushrooms, especially if you're a beginner. Only eat mushrooms that have been positively identified as safe. When in doubt, it's best to be safe than sorry and refrain from consuming unknown mushrooms. Even experienced foragers can make mistakes, so ongoing exploration and knowledge sharing are vital for safe mushroom foraging.

Identifying Mushrooms

Mushroom identification can be rewarding and challenging at the same time. Still, you can confidently distinguish between edible, inedible, and poisonous species with the right approach and knowledge. Here are some tips and techniques for identification.

Study Key Identification Features

Familiarize yourself with the key characteristics of mushrooms, including cap shape, color, texture, gill attachment, spore print color, stem structure, and habitat. Pay close attention to details like the presence of a ring, volva, or distinctive odor.

Take Spore Prints

Taking spore prints is an excellent way to identify mushrooms. To do this, carefully remove the stem from the cap of a mature mushroom and place the cap gills down on a piece of paper or glass. Cover it with a bowl or container and leave it undisturbed for several hours or overnight. The spores will drop and form a pattern, which can help narrow down identification possibilities based on color.

Use Multiple References

You must cross-reference your findings with online resources and reputable websites dedicated to mycology. Online forums and social media groups focused on mushroom identification can also be helpful for getting feedback from experienced foragers and mycologists.

Join Local Mycological Societies

Local mycological societies or clubs are excellent resources for mushroom enthusiasts. These groups sometimes conduct forays, workshops, and educational events led by experienced mycologists. Joining these events gives you more knowledge of local mushroom species and their habitats.

Practice Caution with Look-alikes

Many edible mushrooms have toxic look-alikes, making accurate identification crucial. Always compare the mushrooms you've found with known edible species and their poisonous counterparts. Pay attention to subtle differences in color, texture, odor, and other identifying features.

Start with Easily Identifiable Species

As a beginner, focus on learning a few easily identifiable edible mushrooms first, like chanterelles, morels, or oyster mushrooms. Once you feel confident identifying these species, gradually expand your knowledge to include a wider variety of mushrooms.

Never Eat Unidentified Mushrooms

When in doubt, err on the side of caution and refrain from eating any mushroom you cannot positively identify as safe. Some poisonous mushrooms can cause severe illness or even death, so it's essential to prioritize safety at all times.

Remember, mushroom identification is a skill that develops over time with practice and experience. Using multiple sources for verification, practicing caution, and continuing to learn from experienced foragers and mycologists can make mushroom foraging fun while minimizing the risks.

Safety Considerations

Foraging safely is essential when it comes to mushrooms, not just for your well-being but also for the health of the ecosystem. Remember the features you use for mushroom identification and apply them to keep yourself safe. Here are some one-liners to keep you on track.

- You must always positively identify mushrooms before consuming them.

- Use online resources for confirmation.

- Pay close attention to key identification features, and beware of toxic look-alikes.

- When in doubt, do not consume the mushroom.

- Start with easily identifiable edible mushrooms and gradually expand your knowledge as you gain experience.

- Only consume a mushroom if you are 100% certain of its identity.

- Continuously educate yourself about mushroom identification, toxicity, and safe foraging practices.

- Practice responsible foraging by leaving the environment as you found it.

- Avoid trampling vegetation, disturbing wildlife habitats, or damaging the soil to minimize your impact on the ecosystem.
- Only harvest mushrooms you intend to use, and do so in moderation.
- Avoid over-harvesting and respect natural cycles of growth and reproduction.
- Leave some mushrooms behind to ensure their continued presence in the ecosystem and to support wildlife that depend on them for food and habitat.
- When harvesting mushrooms, cut them at the base of the stem rather than pulling them up. This helps preserve the mycelium and allows the mushroom to regrow.
- Respect any regulations or restrictions on foraging in protected areas like national parks, nature reserves, or private land.
- Always obtain permission before foraging on private property, and adhere to any guidelines provided by landowners or park authorities.
- If you carry any packaging or waste with you during your foraging trip, ensure that you dispose of it responsibly.
- Pack out all trash and leave no trace behind.
- Share your knowledge and enthusiasm for mushroom foraging with others, emphasizing the importance of safety, responsible foraging practices, and environmental stewardship.

Common Edible Mushrooms

Morel Mushrooms *(Morchella spp.)*

Morels are highly prized for their distinctive appearance. They feature a honeycomb-like cap with deep pits and ridges. They vary in color from pale yellow to dark brown and can reach several inches in height.

- **Habitat:** Morels grow in woodlands, particularly around deciduous trees like ash, elm, and oak. They prefer moist soil and are commonly found in early spring after rainfall.
- **Sustainable Harvesting:** When harvesting morels, cut them at the base of the stem instead of pulling them up to preserve the underground mycelium. Leave some mushrooms behind to ensure future growth and sustainability.

Oyster Mushrooms *(Pleurotus ostreatus)*

Oyster mushrooms have a fan or oyster-shaped cap with a whitish to light brown coloration. They typically grow in clusters on dead or dying hardwood trees.

- **Habitat:** They are saprophytic, meaning they feed on dead organic matter. Look for them on hardwood logs, stumps, or fallen branches, especially after periods of rain.

- **Sustainable Harvesting:** Harvest oyster mushrooms by cutting them cleanly at the base of the cluster. Leave some behind to support the decomposition process and allow for future growth.

Shaggy Mane Mushrooms *(Coprinus comatus)*

Shaggy mane mushrooms have tall, cylindrical white caps covered in shaggy scales. As they mature, the caps turn black and liquefy, giving them their distinctive appearance.

- **Habitat:** These mushrooms grow in disturbed areas like lawns, roadsides, or compost piles. They can also be found in grassy fields and meadows.

- **Sustainable Harvesting:** Harvest shaggy mane mushrooms when young and still upright. Avoid harvesting them after they have begun to liquefy, as they become inedible at that stage.

Porcini Mushrooms *(Boletus edulis)*

Porcini mushrooms have a large, thick stem and a broad, convex cap with a brown to reddish-brown coloration.[66]

Porcini mushrooms have a large, thick stem and a broad, convex cap with a brown to reddish-brown coloration. The cap surface is often dry and slightly velvety.

- **Habitat:** Porcini mushrooms form mycorrhizal associations with various tree species, including oak, pine, and birch. They are commonly found in mixed woodlands and coniferous forests.
- **Sustainable Harvesting:** Carefully cut porcini mushrooms at the base of the stem to avoid damaging the mycelium. Harvest selectively and avoid over-harvesting to ensure the continued presence of porcini in the ecosystem.

Maitake Mushrooms *(Grifola frondosa)*

Maitake mushrooms, also known as hen-of-the-woods, have a distinctive frilly or leafy appearance. They have overlapping clusters of fan-shaped caps and range in color from light brown to dark gray.

- **Habitat:** Maitake mushrooms grow at the base of oak trees or on decaying hardwood stumps. They thrive in moist, shaded areas of the forest.
- **Sustainable Harvesting:** Almost every mushroom, including the maitake mushrooms, must be sliced off carefully at the base to avoid damaging nearby mushrooms. Remember to leave some mushrooms behind to support the host tree's health and future growth.

Hen-of-the-Woods Mushrooms *(Grifola frondosa)*

Hen-of-the-woods mushrooms, also known as maitake, have a distinctive frilly or leafy appearance, with overlapping clusters of fan-shaped caps. They range in color from light brown to dark gray.

- **Habitat:** Hen-of-the-woods mushrooms grow at the base of oak trees or on decaying hardwood stumps. They thrive in moist, shaded areas of the forest.
- **Sustainable Harvesting:** When harvesting hen-of-the-woods mushrooms, cut the clusters at the base and leave the mycelium so it can grow back.

Chanterelle Mushrooms *(Cantharellus spp.)*

Chanterelle mushrooms have a funnel-shaped cap with wavy edges and a vibrant golden to orange coloration. They have a mild, fruity aroma and a delicate flavor.

- **Habitat:** Chanterelle mushrooms grow in both deciduous and coniferous forests, often near oak, beech, or pine trees. They prefer well-drained soil and are commonly found in late summer and fall.

- **Sustainable Harvesting:** Always cut at the base and don't damage the mycelium so the mushroom can proliferate further and keep supporting the ecosystem.

Lion's Mane Mushrooms *(Hericium erinaceus)*

Lion's mane mushrooms have a unique appearance, resembling cascading white icicles or pom-poms. They have a mild, seafood-like flavor and a soft, tender texture.

- **Habitat:** Lion's mane mushrooms typically grow on hardwood trees, including oak, maple, and beech. Look for them in late summer or fall, often at the base of trees or on fallen logs.

- **Sustainable Harvesting:** When harvesting lion's mane mushrooms, carefully cut them at the base to avoid damaging the host tree and leave some to support the health of the forest ecosystem.

Black Trumpet Mushrooms *(Craterellus cornucopioides)*

Black trumpet mushrooms have a funnel-shaped cap with a blackish-brown coloration and a delicate, thin texture.[57]

Black trumpet mushrooms have a funnel-shaped cap with a blackish-brown coloration and a delicate, thin texture. They have a rich, earthy flavor and are prized for their culinary versatility.

- **Habitat:** Black trumpet mushrooms often grow in deciduous forests, particularly in rich, moist soil areas. Look for them in late summer or fall, usually associated with beech, oak, or maple trees.

- **Sustainable Harvesting:** Gently cut them at the base of the stem and be mindful of leaving some mushrooms behind.

Yellowfoot Mushrooms *(Cantharellus tubeworms)*

Yellowfoot mushrooms, also known as winter chanterelles, have a slender, trumpet-shaped cap with a bright yellow to orange coloration. They have a fruity aroma and a delicate, nutty flavor.

- **Habitat:** Yellowfoot mushrooms grow in coniferous and deciduous forests, often in mossy areas or along forest edges. They are commonly found in late summer or fall, particularly after periods of rain.

- **Sustainable Harvesting:** Like any other mushroom, you must cut it from the base and leave some untouched for further propagation.

Lobster Mushrooms *(Hypomyces lactifluorum)*

Lobster mushrooms are not a distinct species but a parasitic fungus that colonizes other mushrooms, typically Russula or Lactarius. They have a vibrant red-orange coloration with a lobster-like texture.

- **Habitat:** Lobster mushrooms are often found in mixed woodlands, particularly where Russula or Lactarius mushrooms grow. They can also be found in open fields or grassy areas.

- **Sustainable Harvesting:** Always leave some mushrooms when foraging and make a cut at its stem.

Chicken of the Woods *(Laetiporus sulphureus)*

Chicken of the Woods mushrooms have bright orange to yellow shelves with a soft, spongy texture. They often grow in large clusters on the trunks or branches of living or dead hardwood trees.

- **Habitat:** Chicken of the Woods mushrooms prefers hardwood forests, mainly oak, maple, or beech trees. Wood chips, logs, or stumps are other places where you will find it thriving.

- **Sustainable Harvesting:** When harvesting Chicken of the Woods mushrooms, cut them from the tree or substrate using a knife.

Hedgehog Mushrooms *(Hydnum repandum)*

Hedgehog mushrooms have a convex cap with tooth-like spines underneath instead of gills. They range in color from pale yellow to orange-brown and have a mild, nutty flavor.

- **Habitat:** Hedgehog mushrooms are mycorrhizal and often grow in association with various tree species, including oak, beech, and pine. Look for them in deciduous or mixed forests.

- **Sustainable Harvesting:** Cut them at the stem and use a sharp blade for a clean cut. You should also leave some hedgehog mushrooms so they can grow back into a colony, ready for foraging again in a few weeks.

Puffball Mushrooms *(Calvatia spp.* and *Lycoperdon spp.)*

Puffball mushrooms are round or pear-shaped with a smooth, white-to-brownish outer surface.[58]

Puffball mushrooms are round or pear-shaped with a smooth, white-to-brownish outer surface. When mature, they release a cloud of spores when squeezed or disturbed.

- **Habitat:** Puffball mushrooms are often found in grassy areas, open fields, or woodland edges. They can grow singly or in groups, commonly found in late summer or fall.

- **Sustainable Harvesting:** When harvesting puffball mushrooms, carefully cut them from the ground using a knife. Be sure to harvest them when they are young and firm to avoid consuming mature, spore-filled specimens.

Meadow Mushroom *(Agaricus campestris)*

Meadow mushrooms have a smooth, white-to-light brown cap with pink gills underneath. They have a mild, nutty flavor and are commonly found in grassy areas and meadows.

- **Habitat:** Meadow mushrooms grow in open fields, lawns, pastures, and other grassy areas. They appear after rain or in the early morning dew.
- **Sustainable Harvesting:** When harvesting meadow mushrooms, carefully cut them at the base of the stem to avoid damaging the mycelium. Be sure to identify them to avoid confusion with toxic look-alikes positively.

Wood Blewit *(Clitocybe nuda)*

Wood Blewits have a convex to flattened cap with a smooth texture and lilac to purple-brown coloration. Their crowded gills are pale lilac when young and brownish with age.

- **Habitat:** Wood Blewits are found in mixed woodlands under broad-leaved trees like oaks and beeches. They typically grow in groups or clusters.
- **Sustainable Harvesting:** When harvesting Wood Blewits, cut them at the base of the stem to preserve the mycelium. Avoid damaging the surrounding environment and leave some mushrooms behind to keep the ecosystem undisturbed.

Giant Puffball *(Calvatia gigantea)*

Giant Puffballs are large, round mushrooms with a smooth, white outer surface. They can grow to massive sizes, sometimes reaching diameters of over a foot.

- **Habitat:** Giant Puffballs are typically found in grassy fields, pastures, and open woodlands. They prefer areas with well-drained soil and plenty of sunlight.
- **Sustainable Harvesting:** When harvesting Giant Puffballs, cut them from the ground using a sharp knife. Harvest them when they are still young and firm before they begin to produce spores.

Shiitake Mushroom *(Lentinula edodes)*

Shiitake mushrooms have a brown, umbrella-shaped cap, a meaty texture, and a rich, earthy flavor.[89]

Shiitake mushrooms have a brown, umbrella-shaped cap, a meaty texture, and a rich, earthy flavor. They are commonly used in Asian cuisine and have many culinary applications.

- **Habitat:** Shiitake mushrooms are cultivated commercially but can also be found growing on dead or decaying hardwood trees in forests. They prefer warm, humid environments.

- **Sustainable Harvesting:** When harvesting wild Shiitake mushrooms, look for them on hardwood logs or stumps. As you already know, you have to cut them at the base of the stem and leave budding mushrooms to support the health of the forest ecosystem.

King Bolete *(Boletus edulis)*

King Bolete mushrooms have a large, bulbous cap with a brown to reddish-brown coloration and a thick, meaty texture. They are highly prized for their nutty flavor and culinary versatility.

- **Habitat:** King Bolete mushrooms are mycorrhizal and often grow in association with various tree species, including oak, pine, and birch. They are commonly found in mixed woodlands and coniferous forests.

- **Sustainable Harvesting:** When harvesting King Bolete mushrooms, carefully cut them at the base of the stem to avoid damaging the mycelium. Harvest selectively and leave some mushrooms behind to ensure the continued presence of King Boletes in the ecosystem.

Velvet Pioppini *(Agrocybe aegerita)*

Velvet Pioppini mushrooms have small to medium-sized caps with a dark brown to black coloration and a velvety texture. They have a mild, nutty flavor and are commonly used in Italian cuisine.

- **Habitat:** Velvet Pioppini mushrooms often grow on decaying hardwood logs or stumps, particularly in moist, shaded areas of the forest. They can also be cultivated indoors on supplemented sawdust or compost.

- **Sustainable Harvesting:** When harvesting Velvet Pioppini mushrooms, cut them at the base of the stem to avoid damaging the substrate. Harvest them when young and tender for the best flavor and texture.

Ensure you have a solid grasp of properly identifying wild edible mushrooms before you decide to forage or consume them. If you've just begun foraging, it's best to gather information and knowledge about their proper identification and discuss it with fellow foragers in community groups or online to develop a better understanding. This is necessary as most mushrooms have poisonous look-alikes that can affect your health.

Chapter 6: Cooking Wild Edibles (+ Easy Recipes)

Now that you've learned about the different types of wild edibles, you can use these foraged plants to prepare tasty dishes. This chapter includes cooking tips and easy recipes to enjoy with your family.

You can use these foraged plants to prepare tasty dishes.[60]

Cooking Tips

- Clean the plants after harvesting them to remove debris, insects, and dirt.
- Focus on recipes that highlight the wild, edible flavors.
- Taste the plants before adding them to your recipe. They may have a different texture or flavor and require cooking or blanching.
- Add wild edibles to familiar dishes. For instance, you can add wild berries to your favorite muffin recipes or wild mushrooms to your pasta dish.
- Try different cooking methods to enhance the flavor of the wild edible, such as grilling, roasting, and sautéing.
- Pair the foraged plants with complementary ingredients to balance their bitterness and improve their taste. For instance, add cheese or salad dressings to asparagus or a sugary ingredient to tart berries.

Put your apron on and start preparing tasty dishes.

Foraged Mushroom Risotto

Mushrooms are a great addition to any recipe, giving this risotto dish a delicious and unforgettable taste. They also reduce cancer risks, boost immunity, increase vitamin D levels, and lower blood pressure.

Ingredients:

- 1 pound of wild mushrooms
- 1 cup of grated parmesan cheese
- 1 cup of heavy cream
- 1 ½ cups of your favorite rice brand
- 5 cups of vegetable and chicken stock
- 1 tablespoon of lemon juice
- ¾ cup of dry white wine
- ½ teaspoon of ground pepper
- ½ teaspoon of salt
- 2 fresh thyme sprigs
- 4 minced garlic cloves

- 2 small, minced shallots
- 8 tablespoons of butter
- Fresh minced parsley (optional)

Instructions:

1. Warm the broth in a small saucepan over medium heat.
2. Melt half the butter in a skillet pan over medium heat.
3. Add the shallots and mushrooms and saute for eight minutes or until tender.
4. Add the thyme sprigs, garlic, salt, and pepper, and stir for a minute.
5. Put the mushroom mixture in a bowl and set it aside.
6. Melt the remaining butter in a pan over medium heat.
7. Add the rice and stir for three to four minutes.
8. Add the lemon juice and white wine and let them simmer while stirring until the liquid is absorbed.
9. Add one cup of the chicken or vegetable broth and stir until the broth is absorbed.
10. Add one broth cup at a time and stir for 25 minutes or until the liquid is absorbed.
11. Add the mushroom mixture to the rice and stir to combine them.
12. Stir in the parmesan cheese and cream. Let them cook for five minutes on low heat. The risotto's texture should be creamy but firm.
13. Place the risotto in a bowl, garnish it with fresh parsley, shaved parmesan, and ground pepper, and serve.

Wild Berry Crisp

Enjoy this colorful and tasty dessert after a hearty meal. Berries have many health benefits, such as reducing inflammation, lowering cholesterol, enhancing the skin, and improving the heart's health.

Ingredients:

Filling:

- 1 cup of blackberries
- 1 cup of raspberries
- 2 cups of blueberries
- 2 cups of strawberries (cut in half)
- ¼ cup of flour
- 2 teaspoons of vanilla
- 2 tablespoons of orange juice
- ¼ cup of granulated sugar

Ingredients:

Topping:

- 1 cup of light brown sugar
- 1 ½ cup of all-purpose flour
- 1 cup of cold and diced butter
- 1 ¼ cup of quick oats
- 1 teaspoon of salt

Instructions:

1. Preheat the oven to 350 °F.
2. Grease a 9-by-3-inch pan with nonstick spray.
3. Mix the flour, oats, salt, and sugar in a large bowl.
4. Add the butter to the mixture and combine them with your hand until crumbs are formed.
5. Put the berries in another large bowl and add the vanilla, orange juice, and sugar.
6. Sprinkle the flour over the berries and toss to coat.

7. Put the berry mixture in the greased pan, and then spread the oat mixture evenly to cover it.

8. Leave it in the oven for 45 minutes or until the top turns light yellow.

Root Vegetable Mash

This dish is a great substitute for mashed potatoes as it is creamier and healthier. Root vegetables are high in potassium, manganese, fiber, and vitamins A, B, and C. They boost the immune system, lower blood pressure, and improve blood circulation.

Ingredients:

- 1 small, peeled celeriac cut into 1-inch chunks
- 1 sweet white potato cut into 1-inch chunks
- 2 large, peeled parsnips cut into 1-inch chunks
- 2 cups of rutabaga chunks cut into 1-inch pieces
- 2 chopped cloves garlic
- 2 tablespoons of olive oil
- 2 tablespoons of ghee or butter
- ¼ teaspoons of ground white pepper
- 1 teaspoon salt
- ¼ cup of heavy cream
- 1 ½ teaspoon of fresh and chopped oregano or thyme

Instructions:

1. Boil one-inch water in a large pot fitted with a steamer basket.

2. Add the celeriac and the rutabaga chunks and cover the pot. Let them cook for eight minutes.

3. Add the sweet potato and parsnip chunks and steam for 17 minutes or until the vegetables feel tender.

4. Blend half of the steamed vegetables in a food processor with a steel blade attachment.

5. Melt the butter in a small skillet on low heat.

6. Add the garlic and olive oil and leave them to cook while stirring for 20 seconds or until the garlic turns brown.

7. Add the oregano or thyme, then remove the skillet from the stove.

8. Place half the garlic mixture over the vegetables, add half the salt and pepper and half the cream, and let them puree.

9. Scrape the sides and puree until they are completely smooth.

10. Put the vegetable mash in a bowl.

11. Repeat the previous steps with the remaining salt and pepper, garlic oil, and steamed vegetables.

12. Mix the two batches and serve.

Berry Crumble Bars

This easy recipe is filled with fresh berries for a mouthwatering dessert that your family will love.[61]

This easy recipe is filled with fresh berries for a mouthwatering dessert that your family will love. It is similar to the wild berry crisp recipe but has a few changes.

Ingredients:

- 4 cups raspberries
- 1 large egg
- 1 cup of shortening
- 3 cups of all-purpose flour
- 3 teaspoons of cornstarch
- 1 teaspoon of baking powder
- 1 cup of white sugar
- ½ cup of white sugar
- 1 pinch of ground cinnamon
- 1 pinch of salt

Instructions:

1. Preheat the oven to 375 °F.
2. Grease a 9-by-3-inch pan with nonstick spray.
3. Mix the egg, shortening, ground cinnamon, salt, baking powder, flour, and one cup of sugar in a large bowl until the dough feels crumbly.
4. Spread half the dough in the greased pan.
5. Mix the berries, cornstarch, and ½ cup of sugar in a small bowl, then spread them over the dough in the greased pan.
6. Crumble the other half of the dough over the berries.
7. Bake in the oven for 45 minutes.

Pickled Ramps

Who doesn't love pickles? They are a great addition to any meal, delicious and easy to make. Ramps are high in selenium, chromium, vitamin A, and vitamin C. They boost immunity and reduce the risk of heart disease and cancer.

Tools:

- 2-quart sauce pot
- 3 32-ounce mason jars

Ingredients:

- 1 pound of ramps bulbs
- 2 tablespoons of pickling spice
- 1 ½ cups of rice wine vinegar
- ⅓ cup of sugar
- 1 tablespoon of sea salt
- 3 cups of water

Instructions:

1. Wash the ramps and remove taproots from the leeks, clinging sheaths, and dirt.
2. Remove the leaves, but don't discard them, as they can be pickled.
3. Put the ramp bulbs in the mason jars and leave ½ inch headspace.
4. Leave them until they come to room temperature.

5. Boil the spices, sugar, salt, vinegar, and water in a pot.

6. Pour the boiled mixture over the ramps up to the jars' brim. Make sure it is boiling.

7. Seal jars tightly, then turn them upside down.

8. Leave them to cool down and store them in the fridge. They will last for months.

Nettle Frittata

This cheesy dish is perfect for a nice lunch or dinner with your family. Nettle leaves are both delicious and healthy. They reduce arthritis symptoms, help manage blood sugar, improve prostate health, and aid with respiratory conditions and seasonal allergies.

Ingredients:

- 6 cups of nettle leaves
- 11 large chicken eggs
- 2 minced garlic cloves
- 1 diced yellow or white onion
- ¾ cup of organic sharp cheddar cheese
- ¾ cup of organic sharp cheddar cheese
- 8 ounces of bacon, cut into 1-inch pieces
- Salt and pepper to taste (optional)

Instructions:

1. Preheat the oven to 375 °F.

2. Mix the eggs in a medium-sized bowl, then add the ¾ cup of grated cheese, salt, and pepper (optional). Set the bowl aside.

3. Cook the bacon and diced onions in a small pan over medium-low heat.

4. Stir using a spatula for 15 minutes or until the bacon and onions turn brown.

5. Add the minced garlic and leave them to cook for one minute or until the garlic turns brown.

6. Add the raw nettles to the cooked bacon mixture.

7. Stir the ingredients with a spatula and keep turning the ingredients every 30 seconds for five minutes or until the nettle leaves are cooked.

8. Remove the pan from the stove and distribute the mixture evenly with a spatula on the pan's bottom.
9. Pour the eggs and cheese mixture over the cooked nettles while shaking the pan.
10. Sprinkle the other ¾ cup of cheddar cheese over the raw frittata.
11. Bake the pan in the oven for 15 minutes or until the surface turns golden or light brown.

Potato Frittata

Potatoes are rich in vitamins B6 and C, magnesium, potassium, manganese, and phosphorus.[63]

This recipe is similar to the previous one, except you will use potatoes instead of nettle leaves. Potatoes are rich in vitamins B6 and C, magnesium, potassium, manganese, and phosphorus. They improve digestion and regulate blood sugar levels.

Ingredients:

- ½ pound of potato
- 2 tablespoons of heavy cream
- 8 large eggs
- 4 ounces of grated cheddar cheese
- 2 sliced scallions
- 2 tablespoons of olive oil
- ½ teaspoon of salt
- ¼ teaspoon of paprika (optional)

Instructions:

1. Preheat the oven to 375 °F.
2. Slice the potatoes thinly with a mandoline. You can peel them or leave them unpeeled, whatever you prefer.
3. Pour the olive oil into a baking 12-inch nonstick skillet with a lid.
4. Place the sliced potatoes in an even single layer.
5. Sprinkle the paprika and salt over the potatoes.
6. Cook the pan over medium heat and cover it with a lid for eight minutes or until the potatoes feel tender.
7. While the potatoes are cooking, whisk ¼ teaspoon of salt, cream, eggs, cheddar cheese, and scallions in a large bowl until mixed.
8. Pour the egg mixture over the potatoes after they are cooked.
9. Leave the skillet pan in the oven to bake for 15 minutes or until the frittata is cooked.
10. Cut into slices and serve.

Wild Greens Pesto Pasta

Children and grownups will enjoy this healthy and tasty dish. Wild greens are rich in vitamin C, which is good for your skin, teeth, and gum health and boosts your immunity.

Ingredients:

- 3 cups of shredded brussels sprouts
- 1 pound of orecchiette pasta
- 3 tablespoons of lemon juice
- 2 teaspoons of lemon zest
- 1 teaspoon of divided salt
- 2 garlic cloves
- ¼ cup of extra virgin olive oil
- ¼ cup of nutritional yeast
- ½ cup of divided pine nuts
- ¼ cup of packed basil
- ½ cup of packed arugula
- ½ cup of packed dandelion greens

Instructions:

1. Cook the pasta in salted water following the box's instructions.
2. Take ¼ cup of the pasta water before discarding it, and set it aside.
3. Blend one teaspoon of salt, garlic, olive oil, yeast, ½ cup of pine nuts, basil, arugula, and dandelion greens in a food processor until smooth.
4. Put one tablespoon of olive oil in a large sauté pan and leave it on the stove over medium heat.
5. Add ¼ cup of pine nuts to the sauté pan and toast them for two minutes or until the nuts turn brown.
6. Add a pinch of salt and the shredded Brussels sprouts, and sauté for eight minutes or until they turn brown and tender.
7. Reduce the heat to low, then combine the cooked pasta, ½ teaspoon of salt, lemon juice, lemon zest, and pesto. If the pasta is dry, add water to the pasta.

8. Remove the pan from the stove and put the pasta in a serving bowl.

9. Garnish with pine nuts and basil leaves, and serve.

Dandelion Flower Fritters

Dandelions aren't just pretty flowers. They can also be incorporated into different recipes and have many health benefits. They can reduce inflammation and cholesterol, improve liver health and digestion, protect against cancer, lower blood pressure, and aid with weight loss.

Ingredients:

- 1 cup of freshly picked dandelion flower heads (must be used right after picking)
- 1 inch of cold-pressed coconut oil
- 1 teaspoon of baking powder
- 1 large egg
- 1 cup of milk
- 1 cup of all-purpose or rice flour
- ½ teaspoon of cinnamon
- 1 teaspoon of vanilla
- 2 tablespoons of sugar or honey

Instructions:

1. Mix all the ingredients except for the dandelion heads.
2. Dip the dandelions in the batter.
3. Place the oil in a pan and leave it on the stove over medium heat.
4. Fry the flower side down in the hot oil.
5. Flip and fry more flowers.
6. Drain the flowers on a kitchen towel and serve hot.

Eggs with Wild Onions

Wild onions have many health benefits, such as strengthening the heart muscles and reducing rashes.[63]

Enjoy this tasty and healthy breakfast dish with your family. Wild onions have many health benefits, such as strengthening the heart muscles, reducing rashes, treating menstrual disorders, and relieving inflammation.

Ingredients:

- 6 eggs
- 1 cup of wild onions.
- 2 teaspoons of butter
- 2 tablespoons of water
- Salt and pepper to taste

Instructions:

1. Chop the onions, put them in an iron fryer, then add the water.
2. Cover the fryer and leave the onions to cook until they feel tender.
3. Add the butter and let them melt.
4. Add the eggs, then scramble them.
5. Sprinkle salt and pepper to taste.

Oyster Mushroom Pizza

Who said that pizza can't be healthy? Prepare this pizza dish for your family and friends and enjoy the oyster mushrooms' unique taste and health benefits. They reduce the risk of heart disease and relieve inflammation.

Ingredients:

- 8 ounces of oyster mushrooms
- 1 tablespoon of chopped fresh chives
- ¼ cup of heavy cream
- Sweet paprika
- ½ cup of finely shredded Parmesan cheese
- 1 handful of baby spinach
- Extra-virgin olive oil
- 16-ounce pizza dough
- 1 large minced or pressed garlic clove
- 1 tablespoon unsalted butter
- Salt and pepper

Instructions:

1. Preheat the oven to 500°F for 30 minutes.
2. Melt the butter in a skillet over medium heat.
3. Add the garlic and mushrooms and let them cook while stirring until they feel tender.
4. Sprinkle salt and pepper to taste, then remove the pan from the stove.
5. Roll the dough into a 14-inch circle and place it on a baking sheet.
6. Prick the dough using a fork to prevent bubble formation.
7. Brush the dough with olive oil, evenly spread the mushrooms on top, then scatter the spinach.
8. Sprinkle a pinch of salt and two pinches of black pepper.
9. Add the parmesan cheese and the paprika evenly over the dough.
10. Drizzle half the cream over the dough.

11. Bake the pizza in the oven for ten minutes or until the cheese turns brown and the crust turns golden.

12. Remove the pizza from the oven and drizzle the remaining cream over it.

13. Garnish with chives.

14. Leave it to cool down for five minutes, slice, and serve.

Wild Blueberry Slab Cheesecake

Cheesecake is everyone's favorite dessert."

Cheesecake is everyone's favorite dessert. Enjoy this tasty recipe with your loved ones.

Ingredients:

Jam:

- 2 teaspoons of freshly squeezed lemon juice
- 2 tablespoons of maple syrup
- 3 tablespoons of cane sugar
- 1 ¼ cups of divided wild blueberries

Crust:

- 4 tablespoons of melted butter
- 1 cup of gingersnap cookie crumbs

Filling:

- ½ cup of sour cream
- 2 large eggs
- 1 teaspoon of pure vanilla extract
- 19 ounces of cream cheese
- ⅔ cup of cane sugar
- ¼ cup fresh blueberries (for garnish)

Instructions:

Jam:

1. Put the lemon juice, maple syrup, sugar, and blueberries in a pot and bring to a boil over medium heat.
2. Simmer for 12 minutes while stirring until the berries turn dark and the mixture thickens.
3. Remove the jam from the stove and let it cool. It should be about half a cup.

Crust:

1. Preheat the oven to 350°F.
2. Mix the melted butter with the gingersnap crumbs in a small bowl.
3. Place parchment paper on a 9-by-5-inch loaf pan.
4. Place the melted butter and gingersnap crumbs on the parchment paper and press on them.
5. Bake the crust in the oven for ten minutes and leave it to cool down on a wire rack.

Filling:

1. Reduce the oven temperature to 300°F.
2. Beat the cream cheese and sugar in a stand mixer bowl fitted with a paddle attachment for two minutes or until they turn smooth.
3. Add the vanilla and eggs to the mixture. Stir on low speed or until they are slightly mixed.
4. Remove the paddle attachment, add the sour cream, and stir using a spatula. Don't over-stir.
5. Place the cheesecake filling over the crust after it cools down. Smooth it out using a spatula.

6. Pour the wild blueberry jam over the filling and drag it through the batter with a butter knife.
7. Leave the pan in the oven for 70 minutes. Avoid opening the oven's door while baking.
8. Turn off the oven, open the door, and let the cake cool for 15 minutes while still in the oven to prevent cracking.
9. Remove the pan from the oven and place it on a wire rack until it completely cools.
10. Cover it and leave it in the refrigerator overnight.
11. Garnish with fresh blueberries, cut into small squares, and serve.

Carrot Salad with Wild Blueberries

This healthy salad can be an appetizer served alongside the main course or a light dinner.

Ingredients:

- ½ cup of pineapple pieces
- ⅓ cup of roasted walnuts
- 1 bunch of carrots
- 1 ½ cups of frozen wild blueberries
- 2 teaspoons olive oil
- 1 cup of diced red pepper
- ½ teaspoon of salt
- 4 teaspoons of maple syrup
- Juice of 1 lemon

Instructions:

1. Mix the oil, maple syrup, salt, and pepper with the lemon juice.
2. Add the wild blueberries to the mix and let them defrost.
3. Peel the carrots and slice them into thin pieces.
4. Make eight ribbon-shaped carrots using a potato peeler for garnish.
5. Grease a pan, chop the walnuts, and add them to the pan.
6. Cut the pineapple into small pieces and add them to the chopped walnuts, then add the carrots and mix.

7. Slowly add the blueberry mixture to the pineapple mixture and serve.

Wild Berry Smoothie

Cool down on a hot summer day with this tasty smoothie.

Ingredients:

- 1 ½ cups of fresh or frozen strawberry, blueberry, blackberry, and raspberry
- ¼ teaspoon of vanilla extract
- ¾ cup of orange juice or plain milk
- 1 tablespoon of honey to taste
- Five ice cubes (only if you are using fresh berries)

Instructions:

1. Blend the mixed berries with vanilla, honey, milk, and five ice cubes until smooth.
2. Pour it into a glass and enjoy.

Wild Mushroom Lasagna

Enjoy this smooth and creamy Italian recipe with wild mushrooms' beautiful aroma and flavor.

Ingredients:

- 1 ½ pounds of wild mushrooms
- 1 ounce of dried porcini mushrooms
- ½ cup of extra virgin oil
- ½ cup of flat-leaf chopped parsley
- 5 garlic cloves
- 2 teaspoons of salt
- 4 cups of milk
- 4 tablespoons of flour
- 4 tablespoons of butter
- 1 ½ cup of grated Parmigiano-Reggiano
- 2 boxes of your favorite brand of no-boil lasagna
- ½ pound of diced fresh mozzarella

Instructions:

1. Clean the wild mushrooms with a damp towel.

2. Soak the dried porcini mushrooms in hot water until they feel tender.

3. Remove the mushrooms' long stems and cut them into small cubes.

4. Smash the garlic cloves and put them in a large saucepan.

5. Add the olive oil and simmer for five minutes.

6. Add the mushrooms and salt to the olive oil and saute over medium heat.

7. Cook the mushrooms for 25 minutes and stir frequently.

8. Add the parsley to the cooked mushrooms and saute for an extra five minutes.

9. Prepare the bechamel sauce by melting the butter over medium heat.

10. Add the flour, stir, and leave them to cook for five minutes.

11. Lower the heat and slowly add the milk.

12. Leave them on low heat for 20 minutes and whisk frequently.

13. After the mushrooms are sauteed, remove the large garlic pieces and puree ¼ of the mushroom mixture. The remaining mushrooms will be used in the lasagna.

14. Add the pureed mushrooms to the bechamel and whisk until blended.

15. Preheat the oven to 350°F.

16. Spread half a cup of the mushroom béchamel sauce in a 13- by 9-inch casserole pan.

17. Next, layer with lasagna noodles and add half a cup of bechamel sauce.

18. Sprinkle the sauteed mushrooms on top, and then add the Parmigiano cheese and diced mozzarella.

19. Keep layering the same way until you finish the ingredients.

20. Cover with foil and bake in the oven for 40 minutes.

21. Remove the foil and bake for another 20 minutes.

22. Leave it for 15 minutes to cool down, then serve.

Spring Salad with Edible Flowers

Edible flowers are rich in potassium, phosphorus, magnesium, and other minerals. They are the perfect addition to a spring salad dish.

Ingredients:

- 8 to 10 fresh nasturtium flowers
- 4 handfuls of kale, dandelion greens, lettuce, spinach, arugula, and radicchio (or any green mix of your choice)
- 34 ounces of fresh mozzarella
- ½ diced bell pepper
- 2 large, sliced radishes
- 1 small, chopped tomato

Dressing Ingredients:

- 1 teaspoon of chopped oregano
- ¼ teaspoon of garlic powder
- 1 tablespoon of chopped basil
- 1 ½ tablespoons of fresh lemon juice
- 3 tablespoons of white wine vinegar
- ¼ cup of avocado oil
- Salt and pepper to taste

Instructions:

1. Divide the green mix into two plates.
2. Add the radishes, tomatoes, and bell peppers to each plate.
3. Next, add the flowers and cheese.
4. Whisk the dressing ingredients together in a small dish and drizzle over the salad dishes.

Chickweed Hummus

This hummus salad goes with any dish. It is delicious and filled with many nutrients. Chickweed can reduce inflammation, aid with weight loss, and improve digestion.

Ingredients:

- 2-3 Cups of chopped chickweed
- 1 can of chickpeas drained and rinsed
- ¼ tablespoon of olive oil
- ¾ cup of tahini
- ½ teaspoon of ground cumin
- 1 clove of minced garlic
- ⅛ cup of lemon juice
- Salt to taste
- 1 tablespoon of water

Instructions:

1. Blend the lemon juice and tahini in a food processor for one minute.
2. Add the garlic, salt, cumin, and oil and blend for another minute.
3. Add the chickpeas and blend for one minute.
4. Add the chickweed and blend until smooth.
5. Add the water and store it in the refrigerator.

Root Vegetable Soup

Warm yourself on cold winter nights with this healthy and hearty soup.[66]

Warm yourself on cold winter nights with this healthy and hearty soup.

Ingredients:

Soup:

- 7 cups of vegetable stock or water
- 10 -12 cups of peeled and diced parsnip, carrots, turnip, celery root, and sweet potato
- 1 medium chopped sweet onion
- ⅓ cup of rinsed pearl barley
- 3 minced garlic clove
- 2 tablespoons of butter or olive oil

Seasoning:

- 1 teaspoon of thyme
- 1 teaspoon of salt
- ¼ teaspoon of pepper
- ¼ cup of chopped dill leaves (optional)

Finishers:

- 2 cups of chopped baby spinach
- Garnish with chopped fresh herbs, a drizzle of olive oil, a squeeze of lemon juice, Parmesan cheese, and homemade croutons (optional)

Instructions:

1. Melt the butter or oil in a large soup pot over medium heat.
2. Add the onions and sauté for five minutes.
3. Add the garlic and stir for 30 seconds.
4. Add the root vegetables and stir for 3 minutes.
5. Add the broth or water, thyme, barley, pepper, salt, and dill (optional).
6. Cover the pot and leave the ingredients to boil.
7. Lower the heat and simmer for 40 minutes. Vegetables should feel tender, not soft.
8. Add the spinach and stir for one minute.
9. Season to taste and garnish (optional).
10. Serve with homemade croutons or bread.

Black Walnut Pie

Enjoy this summer dessert with your family and friends. Black walnuts have many health benefits, such as reducing inflammation, lowering the risk of heart disease, and relieving pain.

Ingredients:

- 6 ounces of black walnuts
- 1 teaspoon vanilla extract
- 2 tablespoons of melted butter
- 1 cup of sugar
- 3 eggs
- 1 cup of dark corn syrup
- 1 unbaked deep-dish 9-inch pie crust

Instructions:

1. Preheat the oven to 350 °F.
2. Add the melted butter, eggs, vanilla, sugar, and syrup in a medium bowl and stir with a fork to mix until smooth.
3. Add the black walnuts and stir again.
4. Pour the mixture into the pie crust and bake for 45 to 60 minutes.
5. Let it cool down on a folded kitchen towel for two hours, then serve.

Enjoy these delicious recipes and take advantage of the many health benefits of wild edibles.

Chapter 7: Medicinal Plants of the Midwest

Throughout history, humans have turned to plants for healing.[67]

Throughout history, humans have turned to plants for healing, drawing on the therapeutic properties of herbs, roots, and botanicals to promote health and well-being. This ancient practice laid the foundation of many modern holistic health practices. From traditional herbal remedies to contemporary botanical medicine, the use of plants for healing spans cultures and civilizations.

Since the early ages, plants have been revered for their medicinal properties and spiritual significance in Egypt, China, India, and Greece. Herbal knowledge has been passed down through generations, with healers and shamans harnessing nature's healing power to treat ailments and restore balance to body functions. These early healers viewed plants as sources of physical healing and tools for spiritual growth and transformation.

The concept of using plants for healing has endured through the ages, evolving alongside advancements in science and medicine. In the modern era, botanical medicine includes various practices, from herbalism and aromatherapy to flower essence therapy and phytotherapy. Integrative and complementary therapies, which combine conventional medicine with alternative approaches, are gaining popularity as people seek holistic solutions to their health concerns.

Today, scientific research continues to validate the therapeutic properties of plants, uncovering the biochemical compounds responsible for their healing effects. From anti-inflammatory herbs to adaptogenic plants that support stress resilience, the potential of botanical medicine to promote health and vitality is being increasingly recognized by mainstream medicine.

In a world where chronic stress, environmental toxins, and lifestyle factors lead to several health challenges, the holistic approach of using plants for healing is a pathway to a healthier life.

Medicinal Plant Profiles

Before exploring these medicinal plants, remember that this information is not a substitute for professional medical advice. Always consult a qualified healthcare practitioner before using any plant for medicinal purposes. Avoid self-diagnosis or self-medication, and seek guidance from a healthcare professional for personalized recommendations.

Echinacea *(Echinacea purpurea)*

Echinacea has a long history of use by Native American tribes for immune support and wound healing.[88]

- **Traditional Uses:** Echinacea has a long history of use by Native American tribes for immune support and wound healing. It was commonly used to treat infections, including colds, flu, and respiratory ailments.

- **Therapeutic Properties:** Echinacea has immunomodulatory and anti-inflammatory effects. It stimulates the immune system, helping the body fight off infections and reducing the severity and duration of colds and flu.

Goldenseal *(Hydrastis canadensis)*

- **Traditional Uses:** Goldenseal has been used by Native American tribes for its antimicrobial properties.

- **Therapeutic Properties:** Goldenseal contains berberine, a compound with antimicrobial, anti-inflammatory, and immune-stimulating properties. It is used to support immune function and promote digestive health.

Elderberry *(Sambucus nigra)*

- **Traditional Uses:** Elderberry use in folk medicine for its immune-boosting properties was well known to natives. It was used to treat colds, flu, and respiratory infections.

- **Therapeutic Properties:** It's rich in antioxidants and flavonoids, which support immune function and reduce inflammation.

Milkweed *(Asclepias spp.)*

- **Traditional Uses:** Native American tribes have used Milkweed to treat respiratory ailments, digestive issues, and skin conditions.

- **Therapeutic Properties:** Milkweed contains latex and other compounds with anti-inflammatory and expectorant properties, which can relieve coughs, congestion, and respiratory discomfort.

Wild Bergamot *(Monarda fistulosa)*

- **Traditional Uses:** Wild Bergamot, or bee balm, was used by Native American tribes in medicine and the kitchen for its aromatic and distinct flavor.

- **Therapeutic Properties:** Wild Bergamot contains thymol and other compounds that kill bacteria and reduce inflammation. These compounds also support immune function and soothe digestive discomfort.

Yarrow *(Achillea millefolium)*

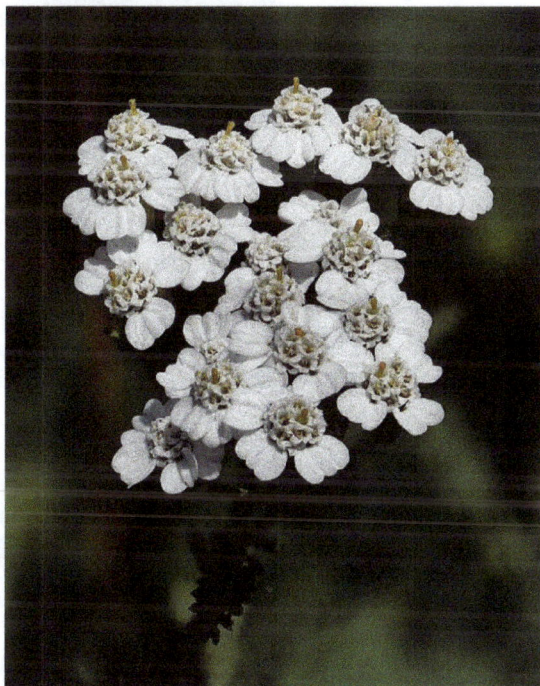

Yarrow has a long history of use in traditional medicine for its medicinal properties.[69]

- **Traditional Uses:** Yarrow has a long history of use in traditional medicine for its medicinal properties.

- **Therapeutic Properties:** Yarrow is used topically to treat wounds, cuts, and bruises. It contains volatile oils, flavonoids, and tannins with antiseptic, anti-inflammatory, and astringent properties.

American Ginseng *(Panax quinquefolius)*

- **Traditional Uses:** American Ginseng has been used for centuries in traditional Chinese and Native American medicine. It promotes vitality, boosts energy, and supports overall health.

- **Therapeutic Properties:** American Ginseng contains ginsenosides, compounds with adaptogenic and immune-modulating effects. These compounds increase stress resilience, enhance cognitive function, and improve immune function.

Wild Ginger *(Asarum canadense)*

- **Traditional Uses:** Native American tribes used wild ginger for its medicinal properties.

- **Therapeutic Properties:** Wild Ginger contains volatile oils and other compounds with anti-inflammatory, analgesic, and antimicrobial properties. Wild ginger can soothe digestive discomfort and relieve respiratory congestion.

Burdock *(Arctium lappa)*

- **Traditional Uses:** Burdock is packed with detoxifying and immune-supportive compounds. It was traditionally used to purify the blood, support liver function, and promote skin health.

- **Therapeutic Properties:** The lignans, polysaccharides, and other compounds have antioxidant, anti-inflammatory, and antimicrobial effects, which can help detoxify, improve digestion, and promote skin health.

St. John's Wort *(Hypericum perforatum)*

- **Traditional Uses:** St. John's Wort has a long history of use in traditional European medicine. At the time, it was a well-known remedy for depression, anxiety, and nerve pain.

- **Therapeutic Properties:** St. John's Wort contains hypericin, which can reduce depression. These properties support mood balance, relieve nervous tension, and improve sleep quality.

Boneset *(Eupatorium perfoliatum)*

- **Traditional Uses:** Boneset has been used in traditional medicine for its fever-reducing and immune-boosting properties.

- **Therapeutic Properties:** Sesquiterpene lactones are the main compound in Boneset, and they have anti-inflammatory and immune-stimulating effects. Whether it's reducing fever, relieving respiratory congestion, or promoting immune function, Boneset can manage it all.

Black Cohosh *(Actaea racemosa)*

- **Traditional Uses:** Black Cohosh was traditionally used to treat menopausal symptoms, menstrual cramps, and rheumatic pain.

- **Therapeutic Properties:** Black Cohosh contains triterpene glycosides, which can alleviate hot flashes, mood swings, and joint pain associated with menopause.

Purple Coneflower *(Echinacea angustifolia)*

- **Traditional Uses:** Purple Coneflower, like other Echinacea species, has been used by Native American tribes to boost the immune system and treat infections like colds, flu, and upper respiratory tract infections.

- **Therapeutic Properties:** Purple Coneflower contains polysaccharides and alkylamides that stimulate the immune system and have anti-inflammatory properties. It can reduce the severity and duration of colds and flu.

Sweet Goldenrod *(Solidago odora)*

- **Traditional Uses:** Sweet Goldenrod was traditionally used to treat digestive issues, urinary tract infections, and respiratory ailments.

- **Therapeutic Properties:** Sweet Goldenrod contains volatile oils and flavonoids, which have diuretic, antimicrobial, and anti-inflammatory properties. It supports urinary tract health, soothes respiratory discomfort, and relieves digestive issues.

Blue Cohosh *(Caulophyllum thalictroides)*

Native American tribes used the plant to support women's health, including menstrual irregularities.[70]

- **Traditional Uses:** Native American tribes used the plant to support women's health, including menstrual irregularities, labor induction, and postpartum recovery.

- **Therapeutic Properties:** Blue Cohosh contains alkaloids and saponins with uterine-stimulating and anti-inflammatory properties. It is still used to regulate menstrual cycles, ease labor pains, and promote healing after childbirth.

Wild Yam *(Dioscorea villosa)*

- **Traditional Uses:** Wild Yam has hormone-balancing and anti-inflammatory properties. It was traditionally used to treat menstrual cramps, menopausal symptoms, and digestive issues.

- **Therapeutic Properties:** Wild Yam contains diosgenin and other steroidal saponins with hormonal and anti-inflammatory effects, which support hormonal balance, relieve menstrual discomfort, and soothe digestive irritation.

Red Clover *(Trifolium pratense)*

- **Traditional Uses:** Red Clover has amazing hormonal-balancing and detoxifying properties. It's used to treat menopausal symptoms, skin conditions, and respiratory issues.

- **Therapeutic Properties:** The isoflavones, flavonoids, and other compounds have estrogenic and anti-inflammatory effects to support hormonal health, improve skin conditions, and soothe respiratory discomfort.

Marshmallow *(Althaea officinalis)*

- **Traditional Uses:** Marshmallow was traditionally used to treat digestive issues, respiratory ailments, and skin irritations.

- **Therapeutic Properties:** Marshmallows contain mucilage and other polysaccharides that form a protective layer in the digestive tract, respiratory system, and skin. This layer formation can soothe irritation, reduce inflammation, and promote healing.

Wild Strawberry *(Fragaria vesca)*

- **Traditional Uses:** Wild Strawberries were a popular traditional medicine for their astringent and anti-inflammatory properties.

- **Therapeutic Properties:** Wild Strawberries contain tannins, flavonoids, and vitamin C, which have astringent, antimicrobial, and anti-inflammatory effects that support digestive health, alleviate diarrhea, and soothe sore throats.

Burdock *(Arctium lappa)*

- **Traditional Uses:** Burdock was traditionally used to purify the blood, support liver function, and promote skin health.

- **Therapeutic Properties:** Burdock's lignans, polysaccharides, and other compounds have antioxidant, anti-inflammatory, and antimicrobial properties. Herbalists recommend it for detoxification, improving digestion, and promoting skin health.

Valerian *(Valeriana officinalis)*

- **Traditional Uses:** Valerian has been used for centuries in traditional medicine as a calming and sedative herb. It was traditionally used to treat insomnia, anxiety, and nervous tension.

- **Therapeutic Properties:** Valerian contains valeric acid that acts on the nervous system to promote relaxation and improve sleep quality. It is often used to relieve insomnia, reduce anxiety, and calm the mind.

Mullein *(Verbascum thapsus)*

- **Traditional Uses:** Mullein has a long history of respiratory-soothing properties and was traditionally used to treat coughs, congestion, and respiratory infections.

- **Therapeutic Properties:** Mullein contains mucilage and saponins with expectorant, demulcent, and antimicrobial properties. Its use can soothe coughs, loosen mucus, and support respiratory health.

Skullcap *(Scutellaria lateriflora)*

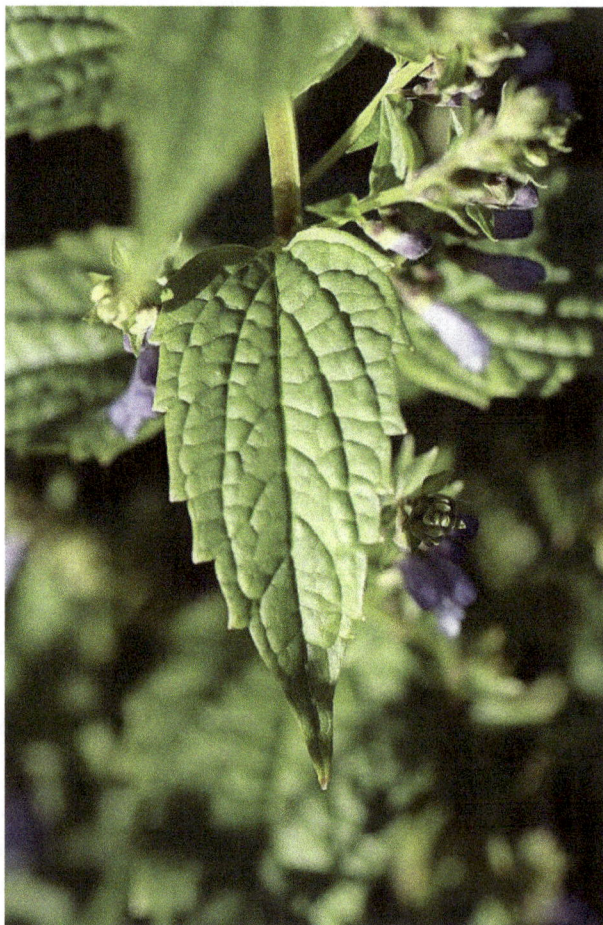

Skullcap has been used in traditional medicine as a nervine tonic and relaxant.[71]

- **Traditional Uses:** Skullcap has been used in traditional medicine as a nervine tonic and relaxant.

- **Therapeutic Properties:** Flavonoids and other compounds act on the nervous system to promote relaxation and reduce anxiety. It calms the mind, improves sleep quality, and supports overall nervous system health.

Catnip *(Nepeta cataria)*

- **Traditional Uses:** Catnip has a long history of use in traditional medicine as a mild sedative and digestive aid.

- **Therapeutic Properties:** Catnip contains nepetalactone and other compounds that act on the nervous system to promote relaxation and reduce anxiety. It is often used to soothe digestive discomfort, relieve insomnia, and calm the mind.

Self-Heal *(Prunella vulgaris)*

- **Traditional Uses:** Self-healing has wound-healing and immune-boosting properties. It was traditionally used to treat cuts, bruises, and infections.

- **Therapeutic Properties:** Self-Heal contains tannins, flavonoids, and other compounds with astringent, antimicrobial, and anti-inflammatory effects. When used topically, it promotes wound healing and supports immune function internally.

Responsible Foraging Practices

Proper Identification

- Always positively identify medicinal plants before harvesting. Use reputable online resources, and, if possible, seek guidance from experienced foragers or herbalists.

- Consider plant characteristics like leaf shape, flower color, growth habits, and habitat.

- Be cautious of toxic look-alikes, as misidentification can have serious consequences.

- Take time to learn about the ecology and life cycle of the plants you intend to forage. Although it will take time to understand their growth patterns and habitat requirements, it will significantly boost your plant identification skills so you can make informed foraging decisions.

Sustainable Foraging Practices

- Harvest only what you need and avoid over-harvesting. Consider the population size, growth rate, and reproductive capacity of the plant species you are harvesting.

- Practice selective harvesting by taking only a portion of the plant and leaving the rest to ensure its survival and reproductive success. Avoid disturbing rare or endangered species.

- Spread your foraging efforts over a wide area to minimize impact on local plant populations.

- Rotate harvesting locations to allow plants time to recover.

Respectful Interaction with Nature

- Treat the natural environment with care and respect. Stay on designated trails and paths to minimize trampling of sensitive habitats and avoid damaging vegetation.

- Likewise, be mindful of nesting birds, burrowing, and other animals affected by your presence.

- Leave no trace – minimize your impact on the environment by packing out any trash or litter, and avoid using plastic bags or containers that can harm wildlife.

Ethical Considerations

- Obtain necessary permits or permissions before foraging on public or private land. Respect landowners' rights and adhere to local regulations regarding foraging and harvesting.

- Avoid foraging in protected areas, nature reserves, or conservation zones where plant collection may be prohibited or restricted.

- Consider the cultural significance of the plants you are harvesting, especially those with historical or ceremonial importance to indigenous communities. Obtain consent and respect traditional knowledge and practices.

You must commit to ongoing education and develop skills in ethical foraging by staying informed about conservation issues, invasive species, and sustainable harvesting techniques. When you've learned, don't keep the information to yourself. Instead, share it with others, promoting a culture of responsible foraging within your community. Encourage others to respect nature and practice ethical foraging principles.

Medicinal Plants in Everyday Life

While many medicinal plants are either dried or eaten fresh, herbalists and traditional plant healers have used various techniques and practices to increase their effectiveness for years. Here are practical tips for incorporating medicinal plants into everyday life, along with various methods for preparation and administration.

Herbal Teas

One of the simplest ways to enjoy the benefits of medicinal plants is by brewing herbal teas."

One of the simplest ways to enjoy the benefits of medicinal plants is by brewing herbal teas. Choose dried or fresh herbs, like chamomile, peppermint, or lemon balm, and steep them in hot water for 5-10 minutes. Strain and enjoy. You can enhance the flavor and medicinal properties of herbal teas by blending different herbs. For example, combine soothing chamomile with invigorating ginger for a calming yet revitalizing blend.

Disclaimer: While herbal teas can be a gentle and enjoyable way to incorporate medicinal plants into your routine, be mindful of potential allergies or interactions. Consult with a healthcare professional if you have any concerns and immediately seek emergency care if you develop any symptoms like rashes, redness of the skin, feeling too hot or cold, or experiencing hot flashes.

Herbal Tinctures

Tinctures are concentrated extracts made by soaking medicinal plants in alcohol or vinegar. They are a convenient and long-lasting way to preserve the medicinal properties of herbs.

To make a tincture, fill a glass jar with chopped or powdered herbs and cover them with alcohol or vinegar. Seal the jar tightly, let it sit for several weeks, and shake it regularly. Strain and store the liquid in a container. Administer tinctures by diluting them in water or juice according to the dosage instructions that the herbalist will recommend after your evaluation. Start with small doses and gradually increase as needed.

Disclaimer: Tinctures are potent extracts and should be used with caution. Always follow dosage recommendations and consult with a healthcare professional before using them, especially if you are pregnant, nursing, or taking medications.

Herbal Infused Oils

Herbal-infused oils are used topically for massage, skincare, and minor ailments. Choose herbs like lavender, calendula, or comfrey, infusing them into carrier oils like olive or coconut oil.

To make an infused oil, fill a glass jar with dried herbs and cover them with carrier oil. Seal the jar and let it sit in a warm, sunny spot for several weeks, shaking it regularly. Strain and store the infused oil in a dark glass bottle. Apply infused oils directly to the skin or use them as a base for homemade salves, creams, or lotions. They can help soothe sore muscles, reduce inflammation, and promote skin health.

Disclaimer: Always perform a patch test before using herbal-infused oils on large areas of skin, especially if you have sensitive skin or allergies. Discontinue use if irritation occurs.

Herbal Poultices and Compresses

Poultices and compresses are external applications of mashed or soaked herbs applied directly to the skin to relieve pain, inflammation, or swelling.

To make a poultice, mash fresh or dried herbs with a mortar and pestle, then apply the mixture directly to the affected area. Cover with a clean cloth or bandage and leave it on for 15-30 minutes.

To make a compress, soak a clean cloth in a strong infusion or decoction of medicinal herbs, then apply it to the affected area. Cover with a warm towel or plastic wrap to retain heat and moisture.

Poultices and compresses can be used to treat bruises, sprains, insect bites, and minor skin irritations. They provide localized relief and promote healing.

Disclaimer: While poultices and compresses can be effective for topical relief, they may not be suitable for all conditions. Consult a healthcare professional for guidance, especially if you have open wounds, infections, or underlying health issues.

Herbal Baths and Steams

Herbal baths and steams offer a relaxing and therapeutic way to absorb herbs' medicinal properties through the skin and respiratory system.

Add dried or fresh herbs to a muslin bag or sachet and hang it under the faucet while filling the bathtub with warm water. Soak in the herbal-infused bath for 15-30 minutes to relax muscles, ease tension, and promote detoxification.

Alternatively, create a steam inhalation by adding herbs to a pot of hot water. Cover your head with a towel and lean over the pot, inhaling the aromatic steam for 5-10 minutes to relieve congestion, sinusitis, or respiratory discomfort.

Disclaimer: Herbal baths and steams can be soothing and refreshing, but they may not be suitable for everyone. Consult a healthcare professional before using them, especially if you have respiratory conditions, allergies, or sensitive skin.

Safety Considerations

When using medicinal plants for health purposes, it's crucial to be aware of potential safety considerations and risks. Here are some key points to keep in mind:

Allergic Reactions

Some people may be allergic to certain medicinal plants, experiencing symptoms like skin rashes, itching, swelling, or difficulty breathing. It's essential to perform a patch test before using a new herb topically, especially if you have sensitive skin or a history of allergies. If you experience any adverse reactions after using a medicinal plant, discontinue use immediately and seek medical attention if symptoms worsen.

Interactions with Medications

Medicinal plants contain active compounds that can interact with medications.[78]

Medicinal plants contain active compounds that can interact with medications, potentially altering their effectiveness or causing adverse reactions.

Certain herbs may interfere with the metabolism of medications in the liver, leading to increased or decreased drug levels in the body.

Always consult with a healthcare professional before using medicinal plants, especially if you are taking prescription medications, to avoid potential interactions.

Toxicity and Side Effects

Some medicinal plants contain toxic compounds that can cause harm if used improperly or in high doses.

It's essential to research the safety profile of each herb before using it, paying attention to potential side effects and contraindications.

Start with small doses and gradually increase as needed, monitoring for any adverse reactions. Discontinue use if you experience any side effects and seek medical advice if necessary.

Pregnancy and Lactation

Pregnant and breastfeeding women should exercise caution when using medicinal plants, as some herbs may have uterine-stimulating or hormonal effects.

Certain herbs are contraindicated during pregnancy and lactation due to the risk of miscarriage, preterm labor, or adverse effects on the infant.

Always consult with a qualified healthcare professional before using medicinal plants during pregnancy or lactation to ensure safety for both mother and baby.

Dosage Guidelines

It's essential to follow recommended dosage guidelines when using medicinal plants to avoid potential toxicity or adverse effects.

Dosage recommendations may vary depending on age, weight, health status, and the specific herb being used.

Consult a qualified healthcare professional or herbalist for personalized dosage recommendations tailored to your needs and circumstances.

Quality and Purity

Ensure medicinal plants are sourced from reputable suppliers who adhere to quality standards and ethical harvesting practices.

Choose organic or sustainably harvested herbs whenever possible to minimize exposure to pesticides, herbicides, and other contaminants.

Consider using standardized herbal products or extracts that undergo quality testing and certification to ensure potency and purity.

Consider consulting a qualified healthcare professional before incorporating new herbs or botanical remedies into your routine, especially if you have underlying health conditions or are taking medications. Safety should always be a top priority when using medicinal plants as part of a holistic approach to health and wellness.

Keep Learning

Here's why continuous education is crucial:

Expanding Knowledge Base

The world of herbalism is vast and diverse, with thousands of plant species and countless traditional uses. Engaging in ongoing learning allows you to expand your knowledge base and discover new herbs, remedies, and therapeutic applications.

There is always more to learn about the botanical world, including plant identification, cultivation techniques, medicinal properties, and traditional wisdom passed down through generations.

Staying Informed

Herbalism is an evolving field, with ongoing research shedding new light on the therapeutic potential of medicinal plants. Staying informed about the latest scientific findings and developments allows practitioners to incorporate evidence-based practices into their approach.

When you keep yourself informed about emerging research, it becomes easier to refine your understanding of herbal medicine, explore innovative approaches, and integrate new insights into your practice of reaping medicinal benefits from these awesome plants.

Empowering Personal Health

Deepening your understanding of medicinal plants empowers you to take control of your health and well-being. By learning how to identify, prepare, and use herbal remedies, you can create personalized wellness routines tailored to your needs.

Education enables you to make informed decisions about your health, choosing natural alternatives that complement conventional treatments and promote holistic wellness.

Cultivating a Lifelong Passion for Nature

Herbalism is not just a practice but a lifelong journey of discovery and connection with nature. Ongoing learning keeps you curious, amazed, and appreciative of the natural world.

By immersing yourself in the study of medicinal plants, you develop a deeper relationship with the earth, cultivating reverence for the healing power of plants and a sense of stewardship for the environment.

Sharing Knowledge

Herbalism is inherently communal, with knowledge passed down through generations and shared among communities. Sharing knowledge and experiences with others will make you a part of the community and camaraderie among herbal enthusiasts, creating opportunities for collaboration, mentorship, and mutual support.

Chapter 8: Living a Foraging Lifestyle

Transform foraging from a hobby into a lifestyle. Commercial farming and food production have a devastating impact on the environment. As the doomsday clock continues to count toward catastrophe, the need for interventions is becoming more pressing. Ethical foraging could be one of the options for sustainability. Unlike monoculture farming, foraging maintains the topsoil nutrients and prevents soil degradation.

Furthermore, foraging institutes an attitude of collaborating with nature instead of fighting against it. Therefore, accepting foraging as a lifestyle takes you a step closer to maintaining and regenerating the planet humanity is collectively

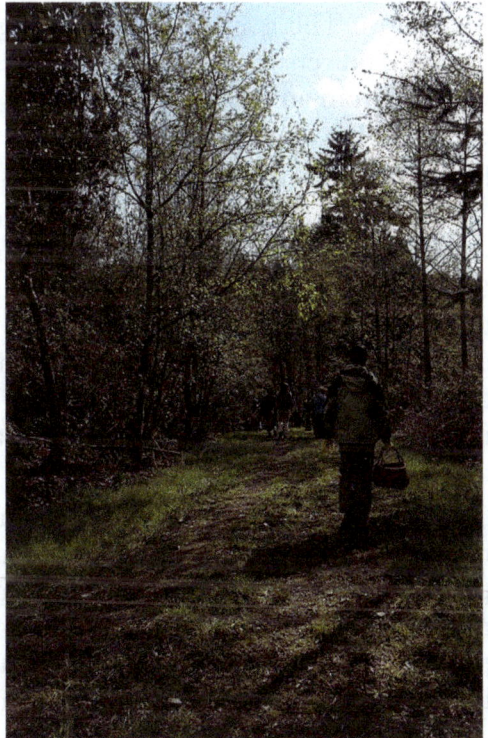

Transform foraging from a hobby into a lifestyle.[74]

destroying. Incorporating foraging into your daily life can be complex, but you can adopt this transformative and sustainable path with a few helpful tips.

Stepping into Sustainability: A Radical Transformation

Foraging is not just a hobby or a practice. Sourcing food in nature is written into your ancient DNA from when humanity understood the intimate relationship with sustenance as a living exchange. Today, the world has reframed nature as something to be conquered or overcome instead of the provider that it is. Therefore, learning sustainable foraging reintroduces you to a transformative relationship with the natural world.

The extreme weather changes common in the Mid-West – and the gorgeous forests and prairies that paint the scenic landscapes – are the perfect introduction to conservation. Ethical foraging promotes sustainability and allows foodies to embark on wonderful culinary adventures. The overlap between foraging and sustainability is wide. To sustain biodiversity and allow for robust foraging, managing the amount you take from an ecosystem is essential. For example, when you collect an edible bush, you could snip off the leaves instead of harvesting the whole plant, letting the plant continue growing.

Foraging requires you to spend time in nature. This is not a passive walk like a hike or finding a high vantage point to admire the view. Foraging causes you to engage with nature more intimately and on its terms. You begin identifying plant life cycles and the issues they experience, like diseases or malnutrition. You experience the relationships that exist between species. Everything in nature is interwoven, so you notice these connections and become aware of the delicate balance that holds fragile networks together.

This transformative awareness aligns you with yourself because you realize that you also fit into the beautiful puzzle of nature. Foraging allows people to awaken to the reality that humans are not fighting against the natural world but are intrinsically a part of it and fully reliant on what it provides. This breeds the gratitude that prompts you to walk more humbly upon the planet, gently placing your feet instead of stomping around and kicking over the furniture.

Foraging is a meditation. All your senses are involved in the activity. You can immerse yourself in the moment whenever you go out to retrieve nature's bounty. From the breeze on your neck in a cold, damp forest to the dirt under your fingernails from searching the soil, foraging connects you with the primal reality hidden deep in your genes.

Sustainability is the realization that you are not doing the planet a favor. A regenerative mindset is crucial for the long-term survival of humanity. The modern consumer culture cannot continue as more resources are buried under the weight of uncontrolled profit. Many can intellectualize the importance of caring for the environment, but the idea seems abstract and distant when you're not directly involved with natural food, from root to table.

Dive into the Natural Flow

Nature works with cycles, which is why straight lines are so rare in the wilderness. Everything has a curve, swirl, or spiral. The moon goes through its phases, and the sun rises and sets, marking the day. The seasons progress, and the colors and sounds of nature shift according to the time of year. When you eat locally, consuming what you forage, your diet adapts to nature's cycles. Eating this way ties you back to how your ancestors ate when they sat around the fire in the Stone Age. That does not mean foraging transports you back in time, but it indicates you are grabbing hold of a powerful, unbroken tradition as old as the human species. Now that civilization has progressed to a place where convenience has skyrocketed, it is time to consider the strain that is put on the environment.

Pollution and unsustainable practices are encouraged by the demand to access the same kinds of food all year round. The transportation and preservation that goes into getting non-indigenous food onto your grocery shelves is shocking. Only a few decades ago, eating out-of-season fruits or vegetables would have been unthinkable because no one had access to them unless they were preserved. The processed reality today has caused people to forget that the same kinds of food do not grow year-round.

Foraging introduces you to the functionality of the wilderness. People frame spring as the time for life to sprout and winter as the season of death. However, when you start mindfully co-existing with nature, you realize that even the coldest times of the year are overflowing with life when you know where to look. Just like you are more active when you are awake during the day than when you go to sleep at night, nature operates according to what is cyclically appropriate.

The disconnect from nature has caused the environmental crisis that society faces today. Taking the small steps to get back in tune with the flow of nature can start with foraging. Understanding the plant world through edible and non-edible frameworks is a great introduction to biodiversity. From this platform, you can start exploring the numerous factors that go into the life cycles of edible plants, starting with the soil, sun, microorganisms, and the wider biome.

The Mid-West is an ideal location to get acquainted with nature because the region embodies extremes. With blazing temperatures in the summer and below-freezing conditions in the winter, the Mid-West introduces all the personality traits of the planet. Each season has its considerations and preparations. The intricacies of how seasons impact the natural world become clear through foraging processes. You realize that the four-season model needs to be revisited to describe the subtle shifts that make an environment unique.

As climate change becomes more apparent and begins affecting ecosystems in unforeseen ways, the need to respond sustainably increases in importance. Foraging shows you the big difference a small interference can make. Understanding this snowball effect could make people more conscious of the dire position human activity is putting on the natural world.

Health and Foraging

Have you ever picked an all-natural candy bar off a tree? Foraging works with whole foods, eliminating many destructive elements related to food processing. The amount of sugar, preservatives, additives, and chemicals involved in neatly packing your food into a brandable container is unimaginable. If people were to step behind the scenes to glimpse into how their food was produced, they would likely be turned off many of their favorite snacks.

When you forage, you collect plants or fungi, including nuts, berries, herbs, and mushrooms. Whole plant foods have a multitude of nutritional benefits. You can get your daily calcium, iron, vitamin D, and B12 requirements from the whole foods you forage. Plants contain phytochemicals, phytonutrients, and fiber, all contributing to your health.

Phytochemicals like carotenoids help strengthen the immune system, prevent lung and prostate cancer, and assist your eyesight. This eye reparative quality of phytochemicals is essential considering the blue-light damage from screens. Other relevant phytochemicals are flavonoids, which can be anti-inflammatory and help fight diabetes. They also offer neuroprotection to maintain a healthy mind.

In addition to the nutrition you'll get from consuming the superfoods you can find in the Mid-West wilderness, foraging requires spending a lot of time in nature. This has remarkable benefits for your mental well-being. When people are in nature, their stress levels are reduced, and they are at a lower risk of developing depression and anxiety. The bustle of the city has many losing their minds. Concrete buildings are like prison cells that keep your psyche trapped in a cycle of distress. Taking the time to forage releases shackles to get the peace of mind you deserve.

Foraging your food puts you in more control. There have been multiple scandals with food companies using dangerous chemicals and processes. In a world of corporate deception, trusting a label may not be enough to control what you consume. When you pick a fruit from a tree, a leaf from a plant, or fungi attached to some bark, you know exactly where the food comes from. You see it in its rawest form before any process has touched it. You monitor the conditions of your food's manufacture because you oversee the sourcing and preservation.

Nutrition is about controlling what goes into your body. People usually think of nutrition as the food you eat, but that view is incomplete. The digestive system is not the only form of consumption. The eyes, ears, and lungs are all portals of consumption. What you see and hear in nature contributes to the health concoction for your well-being. Furthermore, the fresh air you breathe on your foraging journeys is rejuvenating.

Conservation, Community, and Connection

As you connect with nature, you awaken to the fact that you are a part of it. If people are interwoven in nature, it seems logical that building communities should be an extension of foraging. Humanity has always been structured on tribal formats. These have been filtered through various lenses, including religion, political affiliation, and other subcultures. As social primates, people have a biological drive to connect, communicate, and collaborate. To increase the fulfillment you experience and multiply your learning opportunities, it helps you get involved with communities or groups that are like-minded.

Foraging is tied to sustainability and alternative living, where people find methods to co-exist with nature in a mutually beneficial way. Therefore, if you want to get in touch with foraging communities, you can cast a wide net and reach out to groups that cover topics like permaculture, recycling, off-grid living, and conservation. The internet has made finding communities easy. Join groups on social media sites and follow pages related to foraging in the Mid-West. Through these channels, you'll discover events like workshops or classes. These meeting points will help you build a network and to find your tribe.

Conservation and sustainability need widespread action to be effective. Speak to friends and family members to invite them on outings and introduce them to foraging. You can start by preparing people meals with the food you've gathered, and when they comment how delicious it is, you can extend the invitation. People tend to avoid nature because they are accustomed to the convenience of their homes and, by extension, grocery stores. However, their curiosity can come alive once they are reminded of their connection to nature by direct experience.

The human mind evolved within a natural context, so there is a profound sense of peace when you enter what your brain's factory settings are catered to. Unfolding your connection to nature is made more impactful when you do it in a group. Happiness is amplified when it is shared, so spread the message of how foraging can enhance your mental, physical, and social well-being.

The systems currently underpinning the functioning of society are outdated. In the past, they would paint homes with products that had lead in them. Companies would use the same lead paint on children's toys. As research into the impact of lead grew, governmental regulations were instituted to manage the levels of lead in consumer products. Humanity again finds itself in a similar situation where scientists realize that how people consume and treat the planet can no longer be sustained.

Therefore, the systems need a revamp to align with more regenerative practices that can benefit future generations. Building these new systems can start from the ground up. Once consumer demand shifts, the markets and governments will be forced to respond. By growing from a few centralized cells scattered across the globe, the sustainability movement, of which foraging is a subsection, can exponentially spread.

Learning Never Stops

As a forager, no matter how much you expand your knowledge base, there is always more to learn.[75]

When you start the foraging journey, it is easy to think about edible plants as a long list of items you need to catalog and memorize. You may start dreaming about when your catalog will be so extensive that you do not need to add to it. However, nature is nearly infinite. There is always something new to learn or a technique that can make a process easier.

As a forager, no matter how much you expand your knowledge base, there is always more to learn. Being open-minded and teachable can help you drastically improve. When you get around people who know less than you, it's easy to become egotistical in showing off your knowledge, but even the most seemingly ignorant person may have a gem to give you.

To excel at a new sport like golf or a game like chess, you improve faster by facing opponents who are better than you. Strong opponents cause you to practice and focus because you have a measurable goal to pursue by beating them. Spend time with people who have been foraging for decades. Like the chess player who goes up against tougher opponents, spending time with more skilled people will elevate you.

Constantly read and research. When you gain practical and theoretical information, you know the roads to go down to get more knowledge. For example, when you start learning mathematics, you start by counting, which leads to multiplication and division and eventually to advanced calculus. Gaining familiarity with foraging allows you to learn phrases, techniques, and approaches that could assist you in finding more advanced avenues. Your expanding knowledge base will reveal how much you do not know, but you will be aware of what you need to learn.

Incorporating Foraging into Your Diet

When you first start foraging, it's like a hobby. You go out a couple of weekends on some guided tours and immediately eat what you bring back or share it with family and friends. As you progress from a beginner to the intermediate phase, you may start going out and foraging on your own or with a group of friends. Your foraging frequency increases, meaning you will have many more items to work with. A lot of what you gather could go to waste if you do not work strategically. Therefore, you must find ways to incorporate foraging into your diet so that it can work for you and your lifestyle.

The first aspect to consider when increasing the percentage of foraged food in your daily intake is the nutritional value of what you consume. Research which minerals and vitamins the plants and fungi you forage have. This will help guide you on how to include them in your diet and what supplementation you should use if necessary.

The next consideration may be more important than the first. You must ensure that you forage ethically. Although foraging is a natural process that many other animals participate in, if you do it wrong, you can cause further harm, which defeats the purpose of sustainability that foraging promotes. You should never forage on protected grounds because nature reserves are working to maintain ecosystems. Consume responsibly so that you do not exploit the ecosystem and disrupt the area's natural balance. Be mindful of your imprint on nature and align with the principle of leaving no trace. This means that no one should be able to detect that there were humans present because any equipment or products you brought into the forest were left with you.

Since you'll only be able to forage food in season, you must plan your diet around the different seasonal produce you have available. Additionally, you will need to master preservation techniques like drying, canning, and pickling. These natural processing methods are healthier than what you can buy on the shelf. Furthermore, this will allow you to consume out-of-season food and extend the shelf life of what you've gathered.

Get creative with how you prepare food and research the multiple uses of various edible plants. Some of what you collect can be used for oil; others can be dried and enjoyed as tea. When you uncover the numerous ways one item can be used, you can prevent boredom by varying the dishes you prepare. Moreover, you can dive into new tastes on a culinary excursion. Don't stop at the starting line of discovering a plant is edible, but go beyond that to unveil how many different ways you can enjoy it.

Share the Knowledge

Learning should be a flow that constantly progresses. Flowing water can be clean and drinkable, but it can cause diseases and parasites once it stagnates. Knowledge is similar in that when you allow it to stop with you, it dies. Foraging is a path of sustainability, so you are trying to recruit as many people into the lifestyle as possible to act locally against the global environmental catastrophe.

Connection underpins your relationship with nature and your community. Foraging is an activity that can help you bond and build strong relationships because you can spend hours in the forest looking for useful and edible plants. While you teach, you learn at the same time, creating a balanced exercise. Furthermore, you positively reinforce your interactions with the natural world and your loved ones.

Teaching can show you how much you know about a subject. If you can confidently teach, you can rest assured that you've gained significant insight into a given topic. Teaching also helps you to organize and sift through the information you've gathered. So, when you share your information, you internalize it because you get to reprocess it to package the knowledge so an audience can receive it.

Forage with a Purpose

Your love for nature and concern for the environment likely got you interested in foraging. Follow the intuition of love that prompted you to start the journey. There is a reason that foraging and a regenerative lifestyle appeal to you. Often, people's interest reveals their values. Your actions must coincide with your value system to gain true fulfillment in life.

Foraging is less about finding food and more about finding purpose. The lifestyle has values that improve your connection with the planet and its inhabitants. As you continue down your foraging path, you will unlock the magic wrapped in this lifestyle. People have forgotten that nature is their home. When you return to it, you experience that mother's love, like when you are home for the holidays and get a delicious meal. Proceed with passion and curiosity as nature provides for your mind, body, and spirit.

Bonus: Midwest Foraging Calendar

Midwest Foraging Calendar

❄ Winter ❧ Spring ☀ Summer ❦ Fall	Jan	Feb	Mar	Apr	May	Jun	Jul	Aug	Sep	Oct	Nov	Dec
❧ SPRING												
Asparagus				🌱								
Dandelion				🌱								
Lamb's Quarters				🌱								
Sorrel				🌱								
Plantain				🌱								
Chickweed			▇	🌱								
Nettles			▇	▇	🌱							
Purslane				▇	🌱							
Wild Garlic			▇	🌱								
Wood Sorrel			▇	🌱								
Violets			▇	🌱								
Elderflowers				▇	🌱							
Rose Petals				▇	🌱							
Chive Blossoms				▇	🌱							
Johnny-Jump-Up			▇	🌱								
Wild Onions			▇	🌱								
Wild Radishes				▇	🌱							
Wild Sunchokes				🌱								
Wild Strawberries				▇	🌱							

	Winter ❄	Spring 🌱	Summer ☀	Fall 🍂	Jan	Feb	Mar	Apr	May	Jun	Jul	Aug	Sep	Oct	Nov	Dec

🌱 SPRING

	Jan	Feb	Mar	Apr	May	Jun	Jul	Aug	Sep	Oct	Nov	Dec
Wild Sweet Potatoes					🌱							
Wild Turnips				■	🌱							
Wild Yam				■	🌱							
Morel Mushrooms				■	🌱							
Oyster Mushrooms			■	■	🌱							
Shaggy Mane Mushrooms			■	■	🌱							
Porcini Mushrooms					🌱							
Maitake Mushrooms					🌱							
Hen-of-the-Woods Mushrooms					🌱							
Chanterelle Mushrooms					🌱							
Lion's Mane Mushrooms				■	🌱							
Black Trumpet Mushrooms					🌱							
Yellowfoot Mushrooms					🌱							
Puffball Mushrooms				■	🌱							
Meadow Mushroom				■	🌱							
Wood Blewit				■	🌱							
Giant Puffball				■	🌱							
Blue Cohosh				🌱								
Skullcap				■	🌱							
Catnip					🌱							

❄ Winter 🌱 Spring ☀ Summer 🍂 Fall	Jan	Feb	Mar	Apr	May	Jun	Jul	Aug	Sep	Oct	Nov	Dec

🌱 SPRING

	Jan	Feb	Mar	Apr	May	Jun	Jul	Aug	Sep	Oct	Nov	Dec
Catnip					🌱							
Self-Heal				▪	🌱							
Wild Bergamot				▪	🌱							
Wild Ginger				▪	🌱							
Burdock				▪	🌱							
Valerian				▪	🌱							
Mullein				▪	🌱							

☀ SUMMER

	Jan	Feb	Mar	Apr	May	Jun	Jul	Aug	Sep	Oct	Nov	Dec
Blueberries						▪	▪	☀				
Raspberries						▪	▪	☀				
Blackberries						▪	▪	☀				
Juneberries						☀						
Gooseberries						▪	☀					
Chokeberries							▪	☀				
Huckleberries							▪	☀				
Elderberries							▪	☀				
Red							▪	☀				
Mulberries							▪	☀				
Wild Plums								☀				
Wild Potatoes							▪	☀				

☀ SUMMER

	Jan	Feb	Mar	Apr	May	Jun	Jul	Aug	Sep	Oct	Nov	Dec
Wild Carrots							▉	☀				
Wild Parsnips							▉	☀				
Black Walnuts								☀				
Pecans								☀				
Butternuts									☀			
Walnuts									▉	☀		
Pine Nuts									☀			
Wild Mushrooms						☀		▉	☀		☀	
St. John's Wort							▉	▉	☀			
Boneset								☀				
Purple Coneflower						☀		▉	☀			
Sweet Goldenrod								▉	▉	☀		
Red Clover						☀		▉	▉	☀		
Marshmallow							▉	▉	☀			
Wild Strawberry						☀		▉	▉	☀		
Skullcap				▉	▉	☀		▉	▉	☀		
Self-Heal				▉	☀		▉	▉	▉	☀		
Sweet Goldenrod								▉	▉	☀		
Wild Strawberry						☀		▉	▉	☀		
Purple Coneflower						☀		▉	☀			

	Jan	Feb	Mar	Apr	May	Jun	Jul	Aug	Sep	Oct	Nov	Dec
☀ SUMMER												
Bee Balm						☀		☀		☀		
Wild Indigo						☀		☀		☀		
🍂 FALL												
Acorns									🍂		🍂	
Hickory Nuts										🍂		
Filberts										🍂		
Beech Nuts										🍂		
Chestnuts										🍂		
Wild Onions				🍂						🍂	🍂	
Wild Radishes					🍂				🍂		🍂	
Wild Parsnips									🍂		🍂	
Wild Potatoes									🍂		🍂	
Black Walnuts									🍂			
Butternuts									🍂			
Walnuts									🍂			
Pine Nuts									🍂			
Burdock					🍂				🍂			
St. John's Wort									🍂			
Black Cohosh									🍂			
Purple Coneflower						🍂			🍂			

				Jan	Feb	Mar	Apr	May	Jun	Jul	Aug	Sep	Oct	Nov	Dec
❄ Winter	🌱 Spring	☀ Summer	🍁 Fall												

🍁 FALL

	Jan	Feb	Mar	Apr	May	Jun	Jul	Aug	Sep	Oct	Nov	Dec
Sweet Goldenrod								▓	▓	🍁		
Marshmallow							▓	▓	▓	🍁		
Wild Strawberry						🍁		▓	▓	🍁		
Yarrow						🍁		▓	▓	🍁		
Bee Balm						🍁		▓	▓	🍁		

Index: A-Z of Wild Edibles, Mushrooms, and Medicinal Plants

Toxic Plants and Fungi List

Dwarf Ginseng (Panax trifolius)

- **Looks Like:** American Ginseng (Panax quinquefolius)
- **Differentiating Factor:** Dwarf Ginseng has three leaflets per stem, whereas American Ginseng has five.

White Baneberry *(Actaea pachypoda)*

- **Looks Like:** Black Cohosh (Actaea racemosa)
- **Differentiating Factor:** White Baneberry has distinctive white berries with a black dot, while Black Cohosh has white flower spikes.

Red Elderberry *(Sambucus racemosa)*

- **Looks Like:** Elderberries (Sambucus spp.)
- **Differentiating Factor:** Red Elderberry has red berries and reddish-brown stems, while edible elderberries have dark purple to black berries.

Scarlet Pimpernel *(Anagallis arvensis)*

- **Looks Like:** Chickweed (Stellaria media)
- **Differentiating Factor:** Scarlet Pimpernel has small orange-red flowers. However, chickweed has white star-shaped flowers.

Horse Chestnut *(Aesculus hippocastanum)*

- **Looks Like:** Chestnuts (Castanea spp.)
- **Differentiating Factor:** Horse Chestnuts have a spiky husk, and the nuts are often larger and rounder. On the other hand, true chestnuts have a hairier husk and smaller nuts.

Poison Hemlock *(Conium maculatum)*

- **Looks Like:** Wild Carrots (Daucus carota)
- **Differentiating Factor:** Poison Hemlock has smooth, hollow stems with purple spots, while wild carrots have hairy stems and a more carrot-like scent.

False Morel *(Gyromitra spp.)*

- **Looks Like:** Morel Mushrooms (Morchella spp.)

- **Differentiating Factor:** False Morels have irregular, brain-like caps and a more reddish hue, while true Morels have a honeycomb-like structure.

Young Amanita Mushrooms *(Amanita spp.)*

- **Looks Like:** Giant Puffball mushroom (Calvatia gigantea)
- **Differentiating Factor:** Amanita mushrooms start off as small white balls that can be mistaken for puffballs but will develop a cap and stem as they mature. Puffballs are solid white inside.

Poison Hemlock *(Conium maculatum)*

- **Looks Like:** Yarrow (Achillea millefolium)
- **Differentiating Factor:** Poison Hemlock has finely divided leaves similar to carrot leaves and a smooth stem with purple blotches, while yarrow has feathery leaves and lacks blotches on the stem.

Red-Pored Boletes *(Boletus spp.)*

- **Looks Like:** King Bolete (Boletus edulis)
- **Differentiating Factor:** Red-pored boletes have red or orange pores under the cap, which bruise blue. King Boletes have white to yellow pores.

Inedible Cortinarius Species

- **Looks Like:** Wood Blewit (Clitocybe nuda)
- **Differentiating Factor:** Cortinarius species have a rusty brown spore print and the presence of a cortina (web-like veil), while Wood Blewits have a lilac to purple color and a white spore print.

Spurge *(Euphorbia spp.)*

- **Looks Like:** Purslane (Portulaca oleracea)
- **Differentiating Factor:** Spurge exudes a white, milky sap when broken, while Purslane has a clear sap and fleshy, succulent leaves.

White Snakeroot *(Ageratina altissima)*

- **Looks Like:** Boneset (Eupatorium perfoliatum)
- **Differentiating Factor:** White Snakeroot has smooth leaves with serrated edges and no stem-clasping. Boneset leaves are

perfoliate, meaning they wrap around and appear to pierce the stem.

Young Hellebore *(Veratrum spp.)*

- **Looks Like:** Wild Leeks (Allium tricoccum)
- **Differentiating Factor:** Hellebore has pleated leaves and taller growth. However, wild leeks have smooth leaves and a distinct onion/garlic smell.

Water Hemlock *(Cicuta spp.)*

- **Looks Like:** Wild Parsnips (Pastinaca sativa)
- **Differentiating Factor:** Water Hemlock has a cluster of small white flowers and deeply divided leaves with a hollow stem containing a chambered root. On the other hand, wild parsnip has yellow flowers and a non-chambered root.

Foxglove *(Digitalis purpurea)*

- **Looks Like:** Mullein (Verbascum thapsus)
- **Differentiating Factor:** Foxglove has soft, lance-shaped leaves with a prominent flower spike, while mullein has large, woolly leaves and smaller, yellow flowers.

Deadly Nightshade *(Atropa belladonna)*

- **Looks Like:** Black Nightshade (Solanum nigrum)
- **Differentiating Factor:** Deadly nightshade has larger, bell-shaped purple flowers and shiny black berries. However, the black nightshade has small, star-shaped white flowers and matte blackberries.

Death Cap *(Amanita phalloides)*

- **Looks Like:** Meadow Mushroom (Agaricus campestris)
- **Differentiating Factor:** Death Cap has a white cap and gills that do not change color, whereas meadow mushrooms have pink to dark brown gills.

Crown Vetch *(Securigera varia)*

- **Looks Like:** Red Clover (Trifolium pratense)
- **Differentiating Factor:** Crown Vetch has compound leaves with multiple leaflets and a sprawling habit, while red clover has three leaflets per leaf and an upright growth form.

Conclusion

It isn't too difficult to begin a foraging lifestyle in the Midwest. You can start searching for wild edibles, learn from experience, and improve your practices as you go, just like your ancestors at any time. However, why make the same mistakes and risk your health with unripe or poisonous edibles when you can know everything about foraging beforehand?

Here's a brief summary to help you process the exhaustive information in this book so you can lead a risk-free, sustainable life. You started with the basics of foraging, tracing its history in the Indigenous cultures down to its modern developments. Foraging involves taking things from the environment, so the least you can do is respect nature and plant a few seeds along the way.

While you can usually forage with your hands alone, it's better to equip yourself with tools that will greatly simplify the process. Pocket knives and scissors will ensure you don't pull the plants from their roots. You will also need a bag to carry the edibles collected. Don't forget the safety equipment and a first-aid kit.

The type of edibles you can forage is based on seasons. Dandelions and mushrooms bloom in spring, strawberries and walnuts in summertime, pawpaws and blackberries during fall, and oyster mushrooms and winter cress in winter. Then, you learned to recognize the wide range of wild edible plants thriving in the Midwest. There are plantains, asparagus, violets, clovers, blueberries, chestnuts, onions, potatoes, and so much more.

An entire chapter is dedicated to mushrooms, which are plentiful during spring. You learned to distinguish between the edible and poisonous species and explored a few more advanced foraging techniques.

While you can eat most collected edibles as they are, why not make a delicious meal? Many mouthwatering recipes were explained, from the foraged mushroom risotto to the wild greens pesto pasta. Many of the edibles you foraged have medicinal properties that have the power to cure certain diseases and heal deep wounds.

Once you became a master forager, you delved into the advanced strategies of living a sustainable lifestyle based on your newfound skills. Nature has many delicacies to offer throughout the year. By embracing a foraging lifestyle, you can create a sustainable environment in your home and surroundings.

Key Takeaways

- You can forage with nothing but your hands, but the right tools ensure safety for both you and the environment.

- Look for the right kind of edibles at the right time of the year.

- Based on the descriptions in this book, keep the image of the plant you are foraging in your mind's eye so you can locate it better.

If you enjoyed this book, I'd greatly appreciate a review on Amazon because it helps me to create more books that people want. It would mean a lot to hear from you.

To leave a review:

1. Open your camera app.
2. Point your mobile device at the QR code.
3. The review page will appear in your web browser.

Thanks for your support!

Here's another book by Dion Rosser that you might like

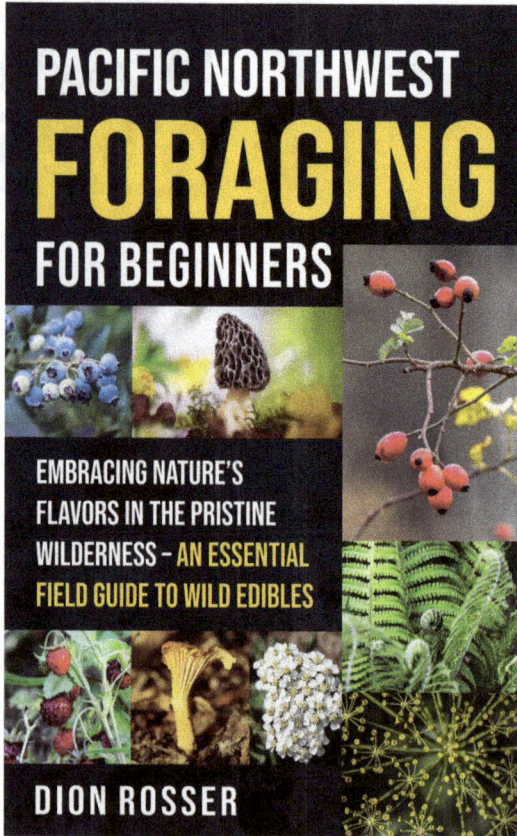

PACIFIC NORTHWEST FORAGING FOR BEGINNERS

EMBRACING NATURE'S FLAVORS IN THE PRISTINE WILDERNESS – AN ESSENTIAL FIELD GUIDE TO WILD EDIBLES

DION ROSSER

References

10 Wild Roots You Can Forage During Wintertime. (2022, January 8). The Northwest ForagerTM. https://thenorthwestforager.com/2022/01/08/10-wild-roots-you-can-forage-during-wintertime/

2023 Great Lakes Foragers Gathering. (2022, October 11). Will Forage for Food. https://willforageforfood.com/2023-great-lakes-foragers-gathering/

3.10 Seasonal Changes in Plants. (n.d.). Flex Books. https://flexbooks.ck12.org/cbook/ck-12-fourth-grade-science/section/3.10/primary/lesson/seasonal-changes-in-plants-scigr4/

A Forager's Checklist for Safe, Sustainable & Ethical Foraging. (2022, January 15). GATHER & GROW. https://gatherandgrow.com/blog/a-foragers-checklist-for-safe-sustainable-amp-ethical-foraging

Aaron and Susan. (2022, May 2). Recipe: stinging nettle frittata. Tyrant Farms. https://www.tyrantfarms.com/recipe-stinging-nettle-frittata/

Aimee. (2019, August 15). Wild Blueberry Slab Cheesecake. Simple Bites. https://simplebites.net/wild-blueberry-slab-cheesecake/

Ajmera, R., & Hill, A. (2018, July 18). Dandelion: Health Benefits and Side Effects. Healthline. https://www.healthline.com/nutrition/dandelion-benefits#weight-loss

Albert, R. (2020, January 2). 6 Benefits of Harvesting Your Timber. Albert Land Management. https://www.albertlandmanagement.com/2020/01/02/6-benefits-of-harvesting-timber/

Asparagus Tops Grocery Lists as Meijer Shoppers Throughout the Midwest Benefit from Michigan Harvest Season. (2021, June 3). Meijer Newsroom. https://newsroom.meijer.com/2021-06-03-Asparagus-Tops-Grocery-Lists-as-

Meijer-Shoppers-Throughout-the-Midwest-Benefit-from-Michigan-Harvest-Season

Avrich, C. (2019, November 8). Root Vegetable Soup. Two Kooks in the Kitchen. https://twokooksinthekitchen.com/root-vegetable-soup-with-barley/#wprm-recipe-container-13427

Baessler, L. (2016, November 12). Picking Blackberries: How And When To Harvest Blackberries. Gardeningknowhow. https://www.gardeningknowhow.com/edible/fruits/blackberries/harvesting-blackberries.htm

Bergo, A. (2013a, February 22). Verdolagas / Purslane. Forager | Chef. https://foragerchef.com/how-to-use-purslane/

Bergo, A. (2013b, March 4). Wild Leeks (Ramps): Harvesting, Sustainability, Cooking and Recipes. Forager | Chef. https://foragerchef.com/a-rite-of-spring-rampsramsonswild-leeks/

Bergo, A. (2018, May 9). Pickled Ramps. Forager | Chef. https://foragerchef.com/the-best-pickled-ramp-recipe/#recipe

Bergo, A. (2022, October 7). Shagbark Hickory Nuts. Forager | Chef. https://foragerchef.com/the-foragers-guide-to-shagbark-hickory-nuts/

Berry Fruits for the Midwest. (n.d.). Zone10.com. https://www.zone10.com/berry-fruits-for-the-midwest.html

Beth. (2021, March 29). Fried Dandelion Flower Fritters (Gluten-Free Optional). Red and Honey. https://redandhoney.com/dandelion-fritters/#wprm-recipe-container-62616

Biodiversity and Ecosystems | U.S. Climate Resilience Toolkit. (2019, October 24). Toolkit.climate.gov. https://toolkit.climate.gov/regions/midwest/biodiversity-and-ecosystems

Black Walnut: Uses, Side Effects, Interactions, Dosage, and Warning. (2019). Webmd.com. https://www.webmd.com/vitamins/ai/ingredientmono-639/black-walnut

BLUEBERRIES BLUEBERRIES. (n.d.). https://www.wifss.ucdavis.edu/wp-content/uploads/2016/10/Blueberries_PDF.pdf

Bouknight, D. C. (2023). Harvest Ramps Responsibly to Enjoy for Many Years to Come. Www.fs.usda.gov. https://www.fs.usda.gov/research/srs/products/compasslive/harvest-ramps-responsibly-enjoy-many-years-come

Brennan, D. (2021, November 9). What Are the Health Benefits of Root Vegetables? WebMD. https://www.webmd.com/diet/what-are-root-vegetables

Burdock: From Seeds To Harvest - Urban Farmer Seeds. (n.d.). Www.ufseeds.com. https://www.ufseeds.com/burdock-seed-to-harvest.html

Calderwood, L., & Tooley, B. (n.d.). Post-Harvest Handling - Cooperative Extension: Maine Wild Blueberries - University of Maine Cooperative Extension. Cooperative Extension: Maine Wild Blueberries. https://extension.umaine.edu/blueberries/post-harvest-handling/

Campell, S., & Yiesla, S. (n.d.). Black raspberry. The Morton Arboretum. https://mortonarb.org/plant-and-protect/trees-and-plants/black-raspberry/#more-information

Casella, P. P. (2019, March 7). Oyster Mushroom Pizza with Paprika, Spinach, and Chives. Thursday Night Pizza. https://www.thursdaynightpizza.com/oyster-mushroom-pizza/#recipe

Chávez Silverman, L. (n.d.). Foraging: Tips To Avoid Poisonous Mushrooms | The Well by Northwell. Thewell.northwell.edu. https://thewell.northwell.edu/healthy-livingfitness/wild-mushroom-foraging-safety

Cherokee Eggs & Wild Onions ~ Traditional Native American Recipe Recipe. (n.d.). SparkRecipes. https://recipes.sparkpeople.com/recipe-detail.asp?recipe=1987069

Common Burdock | Summit County, UT - Official Website. (n.d.). Summitcounty.org. https://summitcounty.org/1250/12150/Common-Burdock

Define Sustainable Agriculture and Discuss How Forages are a Key Component. (2009, May 28). Forage Information System. https://forages.oregonstate.edu/nfgc/eo/onlineforagecurriculum/instructormaterials/availabletopics/introduction/sustainableag

Describe the role of forages in the history of the US. (2009, May 28). Forage Information System. https://forages.oregonstate.edu/nfgc/eo/onlineforagecurriculum/instructormaterials/availabletopics/usforages/role

Diehl, K. (n.d.). Learn How to Harvest and Prepare Nettles. The Spruce Eats. https://www.thespruceeats.com/how-to-harvest-and-prepare-nettles-2952739

Dutta, D. S. S. (2023, November 9). Blooming health: Unfolding the petal-perfect virtues of edible flowers. News-Medical. https://www.news-medical.net/news/20231109/Blooming-health-Unfolding-the-petal-perfect-virtues-of-edible-flowers.aspx

Elisabetta. (2022, November 30). Picking and preserving blueberries. Plantura. https://plantura.garden/uk/fruits/blueberries/picking-blueberries

Elise. (2013, April 30). Chickweed. Elise Krohn | Wild Foods and Medicines. https://wildfoodsandmedicines.com/chickweed/

Esquivel, M. K. (2022). Nutrition Benefits and Considerations for Whole Foods Plant-Based Eating Patterns. American Journal of Lifestyle Medicine, 16(3), 155982762210759. https://doi.org/10.1177/15598276221075992

Everett, W. (2023, March 28). Foraging for Edible Flowers • Insteading. Insteading. https://insteading.com/blog/foraging-for-edible-flowers/

Exploring the Hidden World of Mushrooms: A Comprehensive Guide to Mushroom Anatomy. (n.d.). Stay Wyld Organics. https://staywyldorganics.com/blogs/wyld-trybe/exploring-the-hidden-world-of-mushrooms-a-comprehensive-guide-to-mushroom-anatomy

Five Steps to Harvest Milkweed Seeds This Fall. (n.d.). Agriculture.basf.us. https://agriculture.basf.us/crop-protection/news-events/stories-from-the-field/five-steps-to-harvest-milkweed-seeds-this-fall.html

Forager, F. (2015, May 19). Foraging and Preserving Wild Asparagus. Financial Forager. https://www.financialforager.com/foraging-and-preserving-wild-asparagus/#google_vignette

Foraging Ethics. (n.d.). Wildfoods 4 Wildlife. https://wildfoods4wildlife.com/foraging-safety-ethics/foraging-ethics/

Garlic Mustard: A Delicious Invasive. (2017, May 28). Four Season Foraging. https://www.fourseasonforaging.com/blog/2017/5/28/garlic-mustard-a-delicious-invasive

Garone, S. (2021, April 28). 10 Incredible Edible' Shrooms to Sample. Greatist. https://greatist.com/eat/edible-mushrooms

Geller, J. (2010, April 5). Carrot Salad with Wild Blueberries. Jamie Geller. https://jamiegeller.com/recipes/carrot-salad-with-wild-blueberries/

Gillette, B. (n.d.). How to Grow and Care for Wild Strawberry (Fragaria virginiana). The Spruce. https://www.thespruce.com/wild-strawberry-care-guide-7229743#toc-harvesting-wild-strawberries

Gilmour, L. (2018, February 1). Wild Leeks & Ramps Foraging Guide: How to Find, Sustainably Harvest & Prepare Them. Wild Muskoka Botanicals. https://wildmuskoka.com/blogs/news/harvesting-wild-leeks

Graham, C. (2022, June 6). Foraging: Inside the Modern Resurgence of an Ancient Art. Sustainableamerica.org. https://sustainableamerica.org/blog/foraging-inside-the-modern-resurgence-of-ancient-art/

Grant, A. (2017, May 12). When To Pick Pawpaws: How To Tell If Pawpaw Fruit Is Ripe. Gardeningknowhow. https://www.gardeningknowhow.com/edible/fruits/pawpaw/when-is-pawpaw-fruit-ripe.htm

Grant, A. (2023, January 19). How Do I Harvest Hazelnuts - Tips On Harvesting Hazelnuts From Bushes. Gardening Know How. https://www.gardeningknowhow.com/edible/nut-trees/hazelnut/when-to-harvest-hazelnuts.htm

Grant, B. L. (n.d.-b). StackPath. Www.gardeningknowhow.com. https://www.gardeningknowhow.com/edible/nut-trees/hickory/harvesting-hickory-nuts.htm

Grant, C. (2023, October 25). Foraging Paw Paws. Unruly Gardening. https://unrulygardening.com/foraging-paw-paws/#harvesting-paw-paws

Gregory, H. (2019, December 30). Medicinal Plants, Herbs, and Trees of Missouri | Missouri's Natural Heritage | Washington University in St. Louis. Sites.wustl.edu. https://sites.wustl.edu/monh/medicinal-plants-herbs-and-trees-of-missouri/

,/,<BF<F<Guidance for safe foraging. (n.d.). Food Standards Agency. https://www.food.gov.uk/safety-hygiene/guidance-for-safe-foraging

Hafer, A. (2023, September 9). Essential Foraging Tools: 5 Must-Have Items for Successful Wild Food Harvesting. Outdoors with Bear Grylls. https://outdoors.com/essential-foraging-tools/

Hannah. (2020, June 30). Wild Edible Spotlight Lamb's Quarters. Round the Bend Farm. https://roundthebendfarm.org/2020/06/30/wild-edible-spotlight-lambs-quarters/

Harvesting Elderberry Plants - Stark Bro's. (n.d.). Stark Bro's Nurseries & Orchards Co. https://www.starkbros.com/growing-guide/how-to-grow/berry-plants/elderberry-plants/harvesting

Harvesting morel mushrooms. (n.d.). Extension.umn.edu. https://extension.umn.edu/woodland-ownership/harvesting-morel-mushrooms

Harvesting Nature's Jewels: When Are Huckleberries in Season? - Foraged. (n.d.). Foraged. https://www.foraged.com/blog/when-are-huckleberries-in-season

Harvesting Walnut Trees - Stark Bro's. (n.d.). Stark Bro's Nurseries & Orchards Co. https://www.starkbros.com/growing-guide/how-to-grow/nut-trees/walnut-trees/harvesting

How to Adopt Sustainable Harvesting: Eco-Friendly Practices for the Green Thumb. (n.d.). PictureThis. https://www.picturethisai.com/blog/harvesting-and-post-harvest-handling/How-to-Adopt-Sustainable-Harvesting-Eco-Friendly-Practices-for-the-Green-Thumb.html

How to Harvest Sorrel. (n.d.). Seedsheets. https://seedsheets.com/blogs/howto/how-to-harvest-sorrel

How To Harvest Your Blueberries Without Causing Damage. (n.d.). Plant Me Green. https://www.plantmegreen.com/blogs/news/how-to-harvest-your-blueberries-without-causing-damage

How to Pick and Eat Nettles. (n.d.). Morso Vegan. https://morsovegan.co.uk/blog/nettles

How to Pick Blackberries: Tips for Minimizing Pricks & Getting the Most from Your Harvest. (2018, July 18). Feednflow.com. https://feednflow.com/blog/post/how-to-pick-blackberries

Hughes, M. (n.d.). How to Harvest Black Walnuts and Enjoy Their Delicious Flavor. Better Homes & Gardens. https://www.bhg.com/how-to-harvest-black-walnuts-7571133

Jansen, R. (2019, July 4). Edible Flower Salad. Artful Palate. https://artfulpalate.com/salads/edible-flower-salad/

Jenny. (2023, May 15). How to Properly Harvest and Prepare Morel Mushrooms - Mushroom Appreciation. Www.mushroom-Appreciation.com. https://www.mushroom-appreciation.com/morel-mushrooms-2.html#how-to-properly-pick-morel-mushrooms

Joanne. (2022, December 15). Potato Frittata (Easy Recipe with Best Tips). Fifteen Spatulas. https://www.fifteenspatulas.com/potato-cheddar-frittata/

Kenny, S. (2021, October 20). 7 Tips for Being a Safe and Responsible Forager. Much Better Adventures Magazine; Much Better Adventures Magazine. https://www.muchbetteradventures.com/magazine/7-tips-for-being-a-responsible-forager/

Kootenai National Forest - About the Forest. (2022). Usda.gov. https://www.fs.usda.gov/detail/kootenai/about-forest/?cid=fseprd1120135

Kubala, J. (2021, May 26). 7 Impressive Benefits of Oyster Mushrooms. Healthline. https://www.healthline.com/nutrition/oyster-mushroom-benefits#6.-Other-potential-benefits

Lea. (2022, June 30). Pawpaw: planting, cultivating & harvesting. Plantura. https://plantura.garden/uk/fruits/pawpaw/pawpaw-overview#Harvesting_and_storing_pawpaws

Lorse, S. (2022, September 14). The Dandy Dandelion. Salish Magazine. https://salishmagazine.org/the-dandy-dandelion/

MacKinnon, K., & Wiles, B. (2020, September 17). The beginner's guide to foraging. Backpacker. https://www.backpacker.com/skills/foraging/

Mastering the Art of Foraging and Harvesting Purslane: Expert Tips and Techniques. (n.d.). Discover Real Food in Texas. https://discover.texasrealfood.com/wild-edible-plants/purslane#google_vignette

Mastering the Art of Foraging and Harvesting Wild Strawberries | Expert Tips and Techniques. (n.d.). Discover Real Food in Texas. https://discover.texasrealfood.com/wild-edible-plants/wild-strawberries

Mathes, L. P. (2022, March 5). The Sting of Spring: Stinging Nettles. Edible Madison. https://ediblemadison.com/stories/the-sting-of-spring-stinging-nettles

McDermott, N. (2019, October 11). Black Walnut Pie. Nancie's Table. https://nanciemcdermott.com/black-walnut-pie-for-october-7th/#mv-creation-94-jtr

Meehan, A. (2020, December 28). Chickweed Hummus. Tracks and Roots. https://tracksandroots.com/2020/12/28/chickweed-hummus/

Milkweed Seed Collection. (n.d.). Monarch Joint Venture. https://monarchjointventure.org/get-involved/create-habitat-for-monarchs/milkweed-seed-collection

Miller, L. (2021, June 15). Summer Vegetable Harvest - What Do You Harvest In Summer. Gardeningknowhow. https://www.gardeningknowhow.com/edible/vegetables/vgen/summer-harvest.htm

Nettle Leaf: Health Benefits, Nutrition Facts, and How to Prepare It. (2023, September 7). WebMD. https://www.webmd.com/diet/health-benefits-nettle-leaf

Nolan, T. (2021, October 8). Milkweed Pods: How to Collect and Harvest Milkweed Seeds. Savvy Gardening. https://savvygardening.com/milkweed-pods/

Panoff, L. (2020, April 21). Chickweed: Benefits, Side Effects, Precautions, and Dosage. Healthline; Healthline Media. https://www.healthline.com/nutrition/chickweed-benefits#benefits

Pearce, K. (2023, July 17). 75 Profound And Inspiring Native American Quotes. Mindful Ecotourism. https://www.mindfulecotourism.com/native-american-quotes/

Powell Gardens. (2023, November 2). Midwest Foraging: Winter Guide. Powell Gardens. https://powellgardens.org/midwest-foraging-winter-guide/

Raman, R. (2018, March 14). 7 Health and Nutrition Benefits of Potatoes. Healthline. https://www.healthline.com/nutrition/benefits-of-potatoes#TOC_TITLE_HDR_4

Ramp Season is Here to Stay, For Now - Edible Chicago. (2023, April 8). Edible Chicago. https://www.ediblechicago.com/food-for-thought/ramp-season-is-here-to-stay-for-now/

Regional Morels - Midwest Region - The Great Morel. (n.d.). Www.thegreatmorel.com. https://www.thegreatmorel.com/regional-morels-midwest-region/

RHOADES, J. (n.d.). StackPath. Www.gardeningknowhow.com. https://www.gardeningknowhow.com/ornamental/flowers/sunflower/harvesting-sunflowers.htm

Roy. (2018, July 31). Foraging in Minnesota: Wild Hazelnuts - Never A Goose Chase. Never a Goose Chase. https://neveragoosechase.com/2018/07/31/hazelnuts/

Rozelle, J. (2022, August 23). How to Forage Hazelnuts | Wild + Whole. Www.themeateater.com. https://www.themeateater.com/wild-and-whole/forage/how-to-forage-hazelnuts

Schiller, J. (2016, August 18). The Ultimate Foraging Kit. Outside Online. https://www.outsideonline.com/food/what-gear-do-i-need-foraging/

Seitz, S. (2020, December 19). 39 Different Types of Edible Mushrooms (with Pictures!). Clean Green Simple. https://cleangreensimple.com/article/different-types-of-mushrooms/

Services, H. and S. (n.d.). Wild plants. Www.hss.gov.nt.ca. https://www.hss.gov.nt.ca/en/services/nutritional-food-fact-sheet-series/wild-plants

Shaw, H. (2015, March 19). Foraging for Wild Greens - Identifying Edible Weeds | Hank Shaw. Hunter Angler Gardener Cook. https://honest-food.net/foraging-wild-greens-edible/

Shelly. (2019, May 23). Berry Crisp Recipe. Cookies and Cups. https://cookiesandcups.com/berry-crisp/

Shepard, A. (n.d.). How to Harvest Sunflower Seeds: When to Cut & Dry. American Meadows. https://www.americanmeadows.com/content/wildflowers/how-to/harvest-sunflower-seeds

Shields, T. (n.d.). How To Find and Identify Wild Oyster Mushrooms. FreshCap Mushrooms. https://learn.freshcap.com/tips/oyster-mushroom-identification/

Smith, A. (2019, September 10). The Importance of Sustainable Agriculture. None. https://www.plugandplaytechcenter.com/resources/importance-sustainable-agriculture/

sowtrueseed.com. (n.d.). Planting Guide and Seed Saving Notes for Lambsquarters | Sow True Seed |. Sow True Seed. https://sowtrueseed.com/pages/planting-guide-and-seed-saving-notes-for-lambsquarters

Spritzle, F. (2019, April 24). 11 Reasons Why Berries Are Among the Healthiest Foods on Earth. Healthline. https://www.healthline.com/nutrition/11-reasons-to-eat-berries#TOC_TITLE_HDR_3

Stawarz, S. (2022, February 23). Conservation and Natural Medicines The Doctor is Out... side - The Conservation Foundation. Theconservationfoundation.org. https://theconservationfoundation.org/conservation-natural-medicines/

STEFANONI, A. B. (2015, June 8). Descendants of Family Huckleberry Bush Thrives in Several Places. Joplin Globe. https://www.joplinglobe.com/news/lifestyles/descendants-of-family-huckleberry-bush-thrives-in-several-places/article_a0416b33-8183-5112-b4dc-65147ca55c65.html

Stephanie. (2024, May 2). 10 Tips for Cooking with Wild Edibles. Slow Living Kitchen. https://slowlivingkitchen.com/cooking-with-wild-edibles/

Survival 101: Foraging for Edible Plants. (2014, March 17). Be Prepared - Emergency Essentials. https://www.beprepared.com/blogs/articles/survival-101-foraging-for-edible-plants

Suwak, M. (2023, April 10). How to Harvest Wild Berries: Foraging for Beginners. Gardener's Path. https://gardenerspath.com/how-to/beginners/beginner-foraging-berries/

Talerico, D. (2023, February 1). Chickweed: How to Identify, Harvest, Dry and Use Stellaria Media. Homestead and Chill. https://homesteadandchill.com/chickweed-identify-harvest-dry-use/#h-foraging-and-harvesting-chickweed

Taylor, J. (n.d.). Berry Crumb Bars. Allrecipes. https://www.allrecipes.com/recipe/11050/berry-crumb-bars/

Tripodis, M. (2022, January 6). CW Recipes: Wild Greens Pesto Pasta. Cancer Wellness. https://cancerwellness.com/cw-recipes-wild-greens-pesto-pasta/

TRUSTHERB. (2020, September 28). Health Benefits of Wild Onion also called Jangli Pyaz. Trust the Herb. https://trustherb.com/health-benefits-of-wild-onions/

Twistadmin. (2017, May 9). Mushroom Hunting Safety. Missouri Poison Center. https://missouripoisoncenter.org/mushroom-hunting-safety/

Twitter, & University, F. (2022, September 1). Identifying Wild Mushrooms: A Guide to Edible and Poisonous Mushrooms. Treehugger. https://www.treehugger.com/wild-mushrooms-what-to-eat-what-to-avoid-4864324

uclahealth. (2022, January 24). 7 Health Benefits of Mushrooms. Www.uclahealth.org. https://www.uclahealth.org/news/article/7-health-benefits-of-mushrooms

Uses of Plants. (n.d.). VEDANTU. https://www.vedantu.com/biology/uses-of-plants

Vegan, G.-T. G. (2016, August 25). How to Identify and Pick Oyster Mushrooms. The Greedy Vegan. https://thegreedyvegan.com/how-to-identify-and-pick-oyster-mushrooms/

Webster, K. (2020, November 9). Vegetable Mash. Healthy Seasonal Recipes. https://www.healthyseasonalrecipes.com/vegetable-mash/

WEG, A. (2022, March 7). Everything to Know About Ramps and Why Foodies Say You Need to Stock Up Right Now. Prevention. https://www.prevention.com/food-nutrition/a39315268/what-are-ramps/

Weir, K. (2020, April 1). Nurtured By Nature. American Psychological Association, 51(3), 50. https://www.apa.org/monitor/2020/04/nurtured-nature

Welch, S. (2021, March 30). How to Harvest and Use Dandelion Roots, Leaves and Flowers. Farm and Dairy. https://www.farmanddairy.com/top-stories/how-to-harvest-and-use-dandelion-roots-leaves-and-flowers/656605.html

What Happens to Plants/Trees in the Fall? (2022, November 10). Earth.works. https://earth.works/what-happens-to-plants-trees-in-the-fall/

When to Harvest Summer Vegetables for the Best Flavor: Tips & Tricks. (2022, September 15). Sow Right Seeds. https://sowrightseeds.com/blogs/planters-library/summer-harvest-in-the-vegetable-garden

Why Leaves Change Color. (n.d.). Www.esf.edu. https://www.esf.edu/eis/eis-leaves-color-change.php

Why Plants Grow More in Summer and How to Keep Them Healthy. (2022, September 14). Sow Right Seeds. https://sowrightseeds.com/blogs/planters-library/summer-garden-plant-growth

Wild Berry Smoothie Recipe without Yogurt - Thick Smoothie with Frozen Berries. (n.d.). Foodviva.com. https://foodviva.com/smoothie-recipes/wild-berry-smoothie-recipe/#css_fv_recipe_lplacement

Wild Edible Foods of the Midwest. (2022, May 18). TREEfool. https://treefool.com/midwest-foraging/

Wild garlic. (n.d.). Midwest Invasive Species Information Network. https://www.misin.msu.edu/facts/detail/print.php?id=251.

Wild Mushroom Lasagna. (n.d.). DeLallo. https://www.delallo.com/recipe/wild-mushroom-lasagna/

Wild Mushroom Risotto. (n.d.). The Modern Proper. https://themodernproper.com/wild-mushroom-risotto

Wild Raspberries. (n.d.). Our Tiny Homestead. https://www.ourtinyhomestead.com/wild-raspberries.html

Wood, C. (n.d.). Harvesting Burdock Root Benefits – Digging deep. Www.corinnawood.com. https://www.corinnawood.com/blog/digging-burdock

Image Sources

1   Gordana Adamovic-Mladenovic from Windsor, Canada, CC BY 2.0
    <https://creativecommons.org/licenses/by/2.0>, via Wikimedia Commons:
    https://commons.wikimedia.org/wiki/File:Hand_picking_blueberries.jpg

2   Nick Roux, amendments by LtPowers, CC BY-SA 1.0
    <https://creativecommons.org/licenses/by-sa/1.0>, via Wikimedia Commons:
    https://commons.wikimedia.org/wiki/File:Map-USA-Midwest01.png

3   vastateparksstaff, CC BY 2.0 <https://creativecommons.org/licenses/by/2.0>, via
    Wikimedia Commons:
    https://commons.wikimedia.org/wiki/File:MN_Poison_Hemlock_(14834840320).jpg

4   https://www.pexels.com/photo/footpath-in-forest-20831070/

5   https://www.pexels.com/es-es/foto/creativo-camara-escritorio-cuaderno-4992658/

6   shrinkin'violet from Bristol, UK, CC BY 2.0
    <https://creativecommons.org/licenses/by/2.0>, via Wikimedia Commons:
    https://commons.wikimedia.org/wiki/File:My_trusty_gardening_gloves_%26_secateur
    s_which_need_a_good_clean_by_the_look_of_them_(8711272274).jpg

7   https://www.pexels.com/photo/hiking-boots-and-a-nikon-camera-18236151/

8   KowCFLemont, CC BY-SA 3.0 <https://creativecommons.org/licenses/by-sa/3.0>, via
    Wikimedia Commons: https://commons.wikimedia.org/wiki/File:Plastic_Cover_-
    _Air_tight_for_foods.JPG

9   https://unsplash.com/photos/aerial-photography-of-flowers-at-daytime-TRhGEGdw-
    YY

10 https://www.pexels.com/photo/flat-lay-photography-of-asparagus-351679/

11 American Lotus, CC BY-SA 4.0 <https://creativecommons.org/licenses/by-sa/4.0>,
    via Wikimedia Commons: https://commons.wikimedia.org/wiki/File:Morels.jpg

12 Bruce Marlin, CC BY-SA 2.5 <https://creativecommons.org/licenses/by-sa/2.5>, via Wikimedia Commons: https://commons.wikimedia.org/wiki/File:Black_walnuts.jpg

13 Edal Anton Lefterov, CC BY-SA 3.0 <https://creativecommons.org/licenses/by-sa/3.0>, via Wikimedia Commons: https://commons.wikimedia.org/wiki/File:Sambucus-berries.jpg

14 H. Zell, CC BY-SA 3.0 <https://creativecommons.org/licenses/by-sa/3.0>, via Wikimedia Commons: https://commons.wikimedia.org/wiki/File:Taraxacum_officinale_001.JPG

15 Hugo.arg, CC BY-SA 4.0 <https://creativecommons.org/licenses/by-sa/4.0>, via Wikimedia Commons: https://commons.wikimedia.org/wiki/File:ChenopodiumAlbum001.JPG

16 Ettore Balocchi, CC BY 2.0 <https://creativecommons.org/licenses/by/2.0>, via Wikimedia Commons https://commons.wikimedia.org/wiki/File:Polygonaceae_-_Rumex_crispus-2_%288303634771%29.jpg

17 H. Zell, CC BY-SA 3.0 <https://creativecommons.org/licenses/by-sa/3.0>, via Wikimedia Commons: https://commons.wikimedia.org/wiki/File:Plantago_major_002.JPG

18 https://commons.wikimedia.org/wiki/File:Asparagus_officinalis_Szparag_lekarski_2022-05-22_06.jpg

19 Rasbak, CC BY-SA 3.0 <https://creativecommons.org/licenses/by-sa/3.0>, via Wikimedia Commons: https://commons.wikimedia.org/wiki/File:Stellaria_media_(vogelmuur).jpg

20 Adampauli, CC BY-SA 3.0 DE <https://creativecommons.org/licenses/by-sa/3.0/de/deed.en>, via Wikimedia Commons: https://commons.wikimedia.org/wiki/File:Urtica_dioica_flowers.jpg

21 Attribution-ShareAlike 3.0 Unported, CC BY-SA 3.0 <https://creativecommons.org/licenses/by-sa/3.0/deed.en > https://commons.wikimedia.org/wiki/File:Allium_vineale01.jpg

22 Zachi Evenor, CC BY-SA 4.0 <https://creativecommons.org/licenses/by-sa/4.0>, via Wikimedia Commons: https://commons.wikimedia.org/wiki/File:Oxalis-pes-caprae-36-Zachi-Evenor.jpg

23 Rasbak, CC BY-SA 3.0 <https://creativecommons.org/licenses/by-sa/3.0>, via Wikimedia Commons: https://commons.wikimedia.org/wiki/File:Brassica_rapa_subsp._oleifera,_bladkool_(1).jpg

24 H. Davies[1], CC BY 4.0 <https://creativecommons.org/licenses/by/4.0>, via Wikimedia Commons: https://commons.wikimedia.org/wiki/File:Viola_Cornuta_Horned_Pansy_Mysthical.jpg

25 Otto Sheva2, CC BY-SA 4.0 <https://creativecommons.org/licenses/by-sa/4.0>, via Wikimedia Commons: https://commons.wikimedia.org/wiki/File:Sambucus-nigra_foliage.jpg

26 Nave do Conhecimento, CC0, via Wikimedia Commons: https://commons.wikimedia.org/wiki/File:Rosa_rosa-claro.jpg

27 Vinayaraj, CC BY-SA 4.0 <https://creativecommons.org/licenses/by-sa/4.0>, via Wikimedia Commons: https://commons.wikimedia.org/wiki/File:Trifolium_repens_-_white_clover_on_way_from_Govindghat_to_Gangria_at_Valley_of_Flowers_National_Park_-_during_LGFC_-_VOF_2019_(1).jpg

28 en:User: Laineypaige, CC BY-SA 3.0 <http://creativecommons.org/licenses/by-sa/3.0/>, via Wikimedia Commons: https://commons.wikimedia.org/wiki/File:Daylily_(Hemerocallis_fulva).jpg

29 gailhampshire from Cradley, Malvern, U.K, CC BY 2.0 <https://creativecommons.org/licenses/by/2.0>, via Wikimedia Commons https://commons.wikimedia.org/wiki/File:Monarda_fistulosa_-_Flickr_-_gailhampshire.jpg

30 Kim Hansen, CC BY-SA 3.0 <https://creativecommons.org/licenses/by-sa/3.0>, via Wikimedia Commons: https://commons.wikimedia.org/wiki/File:Viola_tricolor_ssp_tricolor_hald_s%C3%B8_2009-05-13_1.jpg

31 Kazvorpal at English Wikipedia, CC BY-SA 3.0 <https://creativecommons.org/licenses/by-sa/3.0>, via Wikimedia Commons: https://commons.wikimedia.org/wiki/File:Vaccinium.jpg

32 I, Kenraiz, CC BY-SA 3.0 <http://creativecommons.org/licenses/by-sa/3.0/>, via Wikimedia Commons: https://commons.wikimedia.org/wiki/File:Rubus_plicatus_fruit_kz1.jpg

33 H. Zell, CC BY-SA 3.0 <https://creativecommons.org/licenses/by-sa/3.0>, via Wikimedia Commons: https://commons.wikimedia.org/wiki/File:Rubus_fruticosus_003.JPG

34 Alpsdake, CC BY-SA 4.0 <https://creativecommons.org/licenses/by-sa/4.0>, via Wikimedia Commons: https://commons.wikimedia.org/wiki/File:Fragaria_iinumae_(fruits).jpg

35 https://upload.wikimedia.org/wikipedia/commons/8/8d/Amelanchier_alnifolia.jpg

36 Dcrjsr, CC BY 3.0 <https://creativecommons.org/licenses/by/3.0>, via Wikimedia Commons: https://commons.wikimedia.org/wiki/File:Mountain_gooseberry_Ribes_montigenum_berries.jpg

37 Tappinen, CC BY-SA 3.0 <https://creativecommons.org/licenses/by-sa/3.0>, via Wikimedia Commons: https://commons.wikimedia.org/wiki/File:Aronia_mitschurinii_berries.JPG

38 João Medeiros, CC BY 2.0 <https://creativecommons.org/licenses/by/2.0>, via Wikimedia Commons: https://commons.wikimedia.org/wiki/File :Gaylussacia_brasiliensis_fruits.jpg

39 LeonAdler, CC BY-SA 3.0 <https://creativecommons.org/licenses/by-sa/3.0>, via Wikimedia Commons: https://commons.wikimedia.org/wiki/File:Morus_Rubra_ripe_fruit.jpg

40 Dick Culbert from Gibsons, B.C., Canada, CC BY 2.0 <https://creativecommons.org/licenses/by/2.0>, via Wikimedia Commons: https://commons.wikimedia.org/wiki/File:Prunus_americana_(16236067093a).jpg

41 Nikanos, CC BY-SA 2.5 <https://creativecommons.org/licenses/by-sa/2.5>, via Wikimedia Commons: https://commons.wikimedia.org/wiki/File:Quercus_Robur_031.jpg

42 Te Chang, CC BY 4.0 <https://creativecommons.org/licenses/by/4.0>, via Wikimedia Commons: https://commons.wikimedia.org/wiki/File:Carya _texana_in_Houston,_TX_-_leaves_and_fruit.jpg

43 Acabashi, CC BY-SA 4.0 <https://creativecommons.org/licenses/by-sa/4.0>, via Wikimedia Commons: https://commons.wikimedia.org/wiki/File:Hazelnut _Corylus_avellana_at_Woods_Mill,_Sussex_Wildlife_Trust,_England_2.jpg

44 Furudanuki, CC BY-SA 4.0 <https://creativecommons.org/licenses/by-sa/4.0>, via Wikimedia Commons: https://commons.wikimedia.org/wiki/File:Gofukuji_fagus_nuts.jpg

45 Jerry A. Payne, USDA Agricultural Research Service, CC BY 3.0 US <https://creativecommons.org/licenses/by/3.0/us/deed.en>, via Wikimedia Commons: https://commons.wikimedia.org/wiki/File:Carya _illinoinensis_foliagenuts1.jpg

46 https://commons.wikimedia.org/wiki/File:Juglans_nigra_SCA-7685-86.jpg

47 wackybadger, CC BY-SA 2.0 <https://creativecommons.org/licenses/by-sa/2.0>, via Wikimedia Commons https://commons.wikimedia.org/wiki/File:Wild _Leek_(Allium_tricoccum)_-_52351525043.jpg

48 Krzysztof Ziarnek, CC BY-SA 3.0 <http://creativecommons.org/licenses/by-sa/3.0/>, via Wikimedia Commons: https://commons.wikimedia.org/wiki/File:Daucus_carota_inflorescence_kz.jpg

49 MathKnight, CC BY-SA 3.0 <https://creativecommons.org/licenses/by-sa/3.0>, via Wikimedia Commons: https://commons.wikimedia.org/wiki/File:RaphanusRaphanistrum001.jpg

50 H. Zell, CC BY-SA 3.0 <https://creativecommons.org/licenses/by-sa/3.0>, via Wikimedia Commons: https://commons.wikimedia.org/wiki/File:Pastinaca_sativa_003.JPG

51 Jamplevia, CC BY-SA 4.0 <https://creativecommons.org/licenses/by-sa/4.0>, via Wikimedia Commons: https://commons.wikimedia.org/wiki/File:Jerusalem_artichoke_flower.jpg

52 Rasbak, CC BY-SA 3.0 <https://creativecommons.org/licenses/by-sa/3.0>, via Wikimedia Commons: https://commons.wikimedia.org/wiki/File:Brassica_rapa_subsp._oleifera,_bladkool_(1 0).jpg

53 Robert Flogaus-Faust, CC BY 4.0 <https://creativecommons.org/licenses/by/4.0>, via Wikimedia Commons: https://commons.wikimedia.org/wiki/File:Arctium_minus_RF.jpg

54 https://www.pexels.com/photo/shallow-focus-photography-of-orange-and-white-mushrooms-during-daytime-129467/

55 Zhousun21, CC0, via Wikimedia Commons: https://commons.wikimedia.org/wiki/File:Parts_of_a_mushroom.jpg

56 This image was created by user Jimmie Veitch (jimmiev) at Mushroom Observer, a source for mycological images. You can contact this user here.English | español | français | italiano | македонски | മലയാളം | português | +/−, CC BY-SA 3.0 <https://creativecommons.org/licenses/by-sa/3.0>, via Wikimedia Commons: https://commons.wikimedia.org/wiki/File:Boletus_edulis_group_657425.jpg

57 Franck Hidvégi, CC BY-SA 4.0 <https://creativecommons.org/licenses/by-sa/4.0>, via Wikimedia Commons: https://commons.wikimedia.org/wiki/File:Craterellus_cornucopioides_3.jpg

58 MarvinBikolano, CC BY-SA 4.0 <https://creativecommons.org/licenses/by-sa/4.0>, via Wikimedia Commons: https://commons.wikimedia.org/wiki/File:Puffball_Mushroom_in_the_Philippines.jpg

59 Blau de Prússia, CC BY-SA 4.0 <https://creativecommons.org/licenses/by-sa/4.0>, via Wikimedia Commons: https://commons.wikimedia.org/wiki/File:Xiitake_(Lentinula_edodes).jpg

60 https://www.pexels.com/photo/flat-lay-photography-of-vegetable-salad-on-plate-1640777/

61 Neil Conway from Oakland, USA, CC BY 2.0 <https://creativecommons.org/licenses/by/2.0>, via Wikimedia Commons: https://commons.wikimedia.org/wiki/File:Blackberry_Pear_Crumble_(4748443374).jpg

62 Richard Avery, CC BY-SA 4.0 <https://creativecommons.org/licenses/by-sa/4.0>, via Wikimedia Commons: https://commons.wikimedia.org/wiki/File:A_potato_omelette.jpg

63 https://www.pexels.com/photo/scrambled-eggs-with-green-onions-on-black-skillet-pan-5639284/

64 Chris Gladis, CC BY 2.0 <https://creativecommons.org/licenses/by/2.0>, via Wikimedia Commons: https://commons.wikimedia.org/wiki/File:Cheesecake_with_blueberry_topping.jpg

65 Rubyran, CC BY-SA 2.0 <https://creativecommons.org/licenses/by-sa/2.0>, via Wikimedia Commons: https://commons.wikimedia.org/wiki/File:Vegan_mushroom_and_spinach_lasagna.jpg

66 Tiia Monto, CC BY-SA 3.0 <https://creativecommons.org/licenses/by-sa/3.0>, via Wikimedia Commons: https://commons.wikimedia.org/wiki/File:Vegetable_soup_in_Switzerland.jpg

67 Designed by Freepik, https://www.freepik.com/free-photo/high-angle-natural-medicine-wooden-table_8845879.htm#

68 H. Zell, CC BY-SA 3.0 <https://creativecommons.org/licenses/by-sa/3.0>, via Wikimedia Commons: https://commons.wikimedia.org/wiki/File:Echinacea_purpurea_001.JPG

69 Petar Milošević, CC BY-SA 4.0 <https://creativecommons.org/licenses/by-sa/4.0>, via Wikimedia Commons: https://commons.wikimedia.org/wiki/File:Yarrow_(Achillea_millefolium).jpg

70 H. Zell, CC BY-SA 3.0 <https://creativecommons.org/licenses/by-sa/3.0>, via Wikimedia Commons: https://commons.wikimedia.org/wiki/File:Caulophyllum_thalictroides_001.JPG

71 Rolf Engstrand, CC BY-SA 3.0 <https://creativecommons.org/licenses/by-sa/3.0>, via Wikimedia Commons: https://commons.wikimedia.org/wiki/File:Scutellaria_lateriflora_02.JPG

72 https://www.pexels.com/photo/close-up-photo-of-clear-glass-teapot-with-herbal-tea-8330322/

73 https://www.pexels.com/photo/ginkgo-leaf-and-capsules-7615616/

74 Leslie Seaton from Seattle, WA, USA, CC BY 2.0 <https://creativecommons.org/licenses/by/2.0>, via Wikimedia Commons: https://commons.wikimedia.org/wiki/File:Foraging_class_(5733094790).jpg

75 Pavel Hrdlička (Czech Wikipedia user Packa), CC BY-SA 3.0 <https://creativecommons.org/licenses/by-sa/3.0>, via Wikimedia Commons: https://commons.wikimedia.org/wiki/File:Wikitrip_with_botanist_-_%C5%A0pi%C4%8Dat%C3%BD_vrch-Barrandovy_j%C3%A1my_Nature_Monument_5.jpg